# BUFFALO
# SOLDIERS
## ON THE
# COLORADO
# FRONTIER

# Buffalo Soldiers

## ON THE

# Colorado Frontier

NANCY K. WILLIAMS

THE
History
PRESS

Published by The History Press
Charleston, SC
www.historypress.com

*Front cover, top left*: Buffalo Soldier. *National Archives*. *Front cover, top right*: Buffalo Soldier, Twenty-Fifth Infantry. *National Museum of African American History*. *Front cover, center*: Private William Cobbs, Twenty-Fourth Infantry, Colorado, 1894. *History Colorado*. *Front cover, bottom:* Tenth Cavalry, Montana, 1896. *Montana Historical Society*. *Back cover, in text*: Tenth Cavalry, Fort Apache, Arizona, 1887. *University of Arizona Library*. *Back cover, bottom*: Twenty-Fifth Infantry Bicycle Corps, Montana, 1896. *University of Montana Special Collection*.

First published 2021

Manufactured in the United States

ISBN 9781467145442

Library of Congress Control Number: 2020951674

*Notice*: The information in this book is true and complete to the best of our knowledge. It is offered without guarantee on the part of the author or The History Press. The author and The History Press disclaim all liability in connection with the use of this book.

*This book is dedicated to the memory of Tommy.*
*Goodbyes are not forever.*

*If the muse were mine to tempt it*
*And my feeble voice were strong*
*If my tongue were turned to measures,*
*I would sing a stirring song.*
*I would sing a song heroic*
*Of those noble sons of Ham,*
*Of the gallant colored soldiers*
*Who fought for Uncle Sam!*

*—Paul Laurence Dunbar,* The Colored Soldiers, *1894*

# CONTENTS

# Acknowledgements

Though volumes have been written about the Indian Wars and the settlement of the post–Civil War West, the great majority of them overlook the service of the Black troops, the Buffalo Soldiers. There is scant mention in books by well-known historians like George Bird Grinnell in *The Fighting Cheyennes* or Robert Utley in *Frontier Regulars: The United States Army and the Indians, 1866–1891*. In 1967, William Leckie published *The Buffalo Soldiers: A Narrative of the Black Cavalry in the West*, which created the first interest in the Black troops. However, Leckie focused on the Ninth and Tenth Cavalries and their pursuit of Native Americans in Texas and the Southwest. There was little written about the Black infantrymen until Monroe Billington wrote *The Buffalo Soldiers of New Mexico: 1866–1900*. There are no books about the conflicts of the Buffalo Soldiers with the Utes in the Rocky Mountains or their fierce battles with the Cheyenne, Arapaho, and Sioux on the plains of Colorado.

Much appreciation goes to the regional historical societies and librarians for information about the Buffalo Soldiers who served in their areas. Their collections of bullets, arrowheads, cavalry buttons, and artifacts gathered at battle sites and abandoned villages are remnants of that turbulent time.

My thanks to History Colorado, the White River Museum in Meeker, the Ute Indian Museum, and the Fort Garland Museum.

Thank you to Tom Williams, whose skill with the camera captured the lonely battlefields where the ghosts of men who fought still linger.

A special thanks to Artie Crisp, senior acquisitions editor at The History Press.

# INTRODUCTION

D uring his years enslaved, he'd never been allowed to touch a gun, and now that he was a free man, this new Ninth Cavalry recruit had his own guns and was going "out West," where he'd be "shootin' Injuns." After the Civil War ended, he hadn't found work as a field hand or laborer because the boll weevil had chewed through the cotton crop, the fields had been destroyed by the Yankees, and the corn had withered in a drought. He needed work so he'd have money for food and a place to live.

A second young Black man had been unsuccessful in finding any kind of job in the North, and he was living in a shanty town on the outskirts of Philadelphia. After the end of the war, so many Black people traveled north that the competition for work was fierce. His future looked bleak until he heard about the army and thought that might be an answer. He didn't rush to join but talked to the recruiter and learned that enlisted men would be taught to read and write. That decided it for him, and he made his mark, a big *X*, on the enlistment papers. Now all he had to think about was that horse he would learn to ride.

The third Black man was a Civil War veteran who was no longer welcome in the South, where he'd been born into slavery. He'd run away from a plantation when the first Confederate volley started the Civil War and joined the First Infantry in New Orleans. He'd learned about war as he fought with other Black soldiers in the United States Colored Troops (USCT), one of 186,000 slaves and freedmen who'd enlisted in the Union army. When the war ended, he'd returned to the Reconstruction South to face the hatred and retaliation of angry, defeated Confederates. After being dragged out of his cabin one night and beaten by a gang, he fled to the army recruiter. He knew how to shoot a gun and fight, and he was welcomed into the Tenth Cavalry. He'd soon be going west, where he'd fight Indians and chase outlaws.

These three young Black men had different stories, but they shared some things in common. Now that they were free, they needed to earn a living, they wanted to learn to read and write, and they wanted the opportunity to show that they could become good citizens. The Emancipation Proclamation and the passage of the Thirteenth Amendment had freed enslaved Black people, but neither showed them how to survive with their new freedom. When the Civil War ended, there were about one million surviving soldiers as the army began rapid demobilization, sending battle-weary veterans home. Just one year after the end of the Civil War, the army had only 11,000 soldiers, just when it needed the largest peacetime military in history. Troops were essential to maintain law and order, supervise Reconstruction in the South, patrol the Mexican border for revolutionaries and outlaws, and deal with the "Indian Problem" in the West. Attacks by the Plains tribes were taking a huge toll on lives and property, hampering westward expansion, and slowing the nation's growth. Congress appropriated barely enough cash to build additional forts, but the small, demobilized army didn't have enough soldiers to man these forts, patrol the vast prairies, or protect settlers and travelers.

To meet the acute need for troops, Congress passed the Army Organization Act, authorizing the formation of six all-Black regiments in July 1866 and providing an opportunity for former slaves and USCT veterans. In the army, a man would earn thirteen dollars a month, the same pay as a white soldier; plus food, clothes, and shelter were provided. This was an opportunity with the promise of a future.

Recruitment began quickly, units were formed, and training started. The young recruits swiftly became toughened soldiers, serving proudly in the West, pursuing the Comanches and Kiowa in Texas, and chasing outlaws and bandits along the Rio Grande. They fought Apaches in Arizona and New Mexico and subdued the Utes of Colorado. During the Indian Wars from 1861 to 1898, there were about 26,000 men in the army, with 12,500 Black soldiers fighting on the frontier. Of every 5 cavalrymen, 1 was Black, and 8 to 10 percent of the infantry soldiers were Black. In the West, the two Black cavalry regiments made up 20 percent of the mounted troops

For 30 years, Black soldiers represented more than 10 percent of the army's strength in the West, and in some areas, they made up more than half the military force. Because the Buffalo Soldiers are rarely mentioned in the pages of history books, many people will be surprised to learn that they served on the western frontier from the Canadian border to Mexico and from the Missouri River to the Pacific Ocean. By 1898, when they boarded ships for Cuba to fight in the Spanish-American War, Black soldiers had served in nearly all of the western states and territories.

# 1

# SAND CREEK IGNITES
# THE COLORADO WAR

The end of the Civil War in 1865 brought a flood of immigrant wagon trains pouring across the Colorado plains, infuriating the Cheyenne and Arapaho, who mistakenly thought their attacks had driven out the soldiers and settlers and stopped the invasion of their lands. As travelers crossed the prime buffalo country along the Smoky Hill Trail, a main road to Denver, and the Overland Trail, a connection to the Oregon Trail, they were often set upon by large war parties. Angry, frightened Colorado citizens demanded action. Terrorized farmers and ranchers moved their families into Denver as the deadly raids on isolated homesteads on the plains increased. There was little peace of mind in the territorial capital, where everyone was afraid that the tribes were gathering to overrun the town. People clamored for a volunteer militia that could pursue the Indians and drive them completely out of the territory. A full-page editorial in the *Rocky Mountain News* called for "the extermination of the red devils" and urged readers to "take a few months off and dedicate that time to wiping out the Indians."

Governor Gilpin's call for volunteers brought shopkeepers, tavern owners, drifters, and ranch hands to enlist in the First Colorado Volunteer Infantry Regiment, with Major John Chivington in command. Addressing a gathering of church deacons, Chivington, a Methodist minister, declared, "The Cheyenne will have to be soundly whipped—or completely wiped out—before they will be quiet. It simply is not possible for Indians to obey or understand a treaty. The only thing to do is kill them....It's the only way we will ever have peace and quiet in Colorado."

During the summer of 1864, there were more Cheyenne attacks on homesteads and ranches near Denver. On June 11, 1864, the Hungate family, Nathan and his wife, Ellen, their six-year-old daughter, and six-month-old baby, were killed at their small homestead southeast of Denver. Their mutilated bodies were put on public display in Denver, horrifying and infuriating the local citizens. The public was inflamed and eager to "kill the Indians" or drive them out of the Colorado Territory. In August, Governor Evans, who was strongly anti–Native American, issued a proclamation authorizing "all citizens of Colorado…to go in pursuit of all hostile Indians [and] kill and destroy all enemies of the country." Then he ordered "friendly" Indians to go to certain forts for their "safety and protection," and those who refused would be viewed as "hostile," to be "pursued and destroyed." Evans organized a second cavalry unit, the Third Colorado Volunteers, who signed on for 100 days to fight the Cheyenne. Commanded by Chivington, this unit was scornfully dubbed the "Bloodless Third" because it hadn't had any battles.

In September, a group of Cheyenne and Arapahoe chiefs, led by Black Kettle, met with Governor Evans to develop a peace plan. Evans didn't offer them any hope, saying he "was in no condition" to make a treaty, and his soldiers "were preparing for the fight." The discouraged Indians were sent to Fort Lyon for protection, but the new commander, Major Scott Anthony, an anti-Indian ally of Chivington, sent them west to camp at Sand Creek. He assured Black Kettle and Arapaho peace chief Left Hand and their large bands of warriors and their families that they would be safe there. Then he sent a messenger to notify Chivington of the Indians' location at Sand Creek.

In the predawn hours of November 29, 1864, Major Chivington and 700 troops of the First and Third Colorado Cavalry attacked the sleeping Indian camp at Sand Creek. The troops dashed through the village shooting into the tipis of the sleeping Native Americans. As the terrified men, women, and children scattered in all directions, looking for a place to hide on the treeless plain, they were chased down by the mounted militia and shot. Some tried to hide under the overhanging banks of Sand Creek, but the troopers pursued them, slaughtering women, children, and babies without mercy. Indians who were trying to surrender were cut down. Black Kettle was shot near his tipi, where he was flying a white flag of truce beside a giant American flag that President Lincoln had given him. After shooting every Indian they saw, the Colorado Volunteers prowled through the demolished camp, stabbing and killing the wounded, even small children and toddlers, scalping the dead, and mutilating their bodies. They took no prisoners, then burned the tipis, and destroyed the camp.

At the time of this attack at Sand Creek, there were approximately 650 Indians in the camp, as most warriors had gone hunting, leaving only a few old men behind. Historians estimate that approximately 230 people were massacred, and over half were women and children. Black Kettle was wounded but escaped with his wife. Left Hand got away but was severely wounded and was cared for by the Sioux until he died from his wounds. White Antelope, who longed for peace for his people, was killed at Sand Creek. Some of the other survivors of the massacre fled north to the Republican River, where they joined a large body of Cheyenne.

Chivington and the Colorado Volunteers returned triumphantly to Denver, where everyone turned out to cheer them. They paraded through the streets proudly displaying their battle trophies of scalps and body parts, even male and female genitalia. Some Volunteers showed off their gruesome prizes at popular saloons and took the stage at a local theater to display these horrible remnants of the slaughter.

The victory of the Volunteers, while initially praised, was soon condemned as the atrocities of the massacre emerged. Within a few weeks, witnesses began telling their stories, and the truth about the attack on these peace-seeking Indians became obvious. Accounts of the militia's brutality—Volunteers bashing babies' brains out and slashing off ears, fingers, and noses for souvenir ornaments; a trooper who shot a toddler who was running away; and young children slashed to pieces—all aroused the nation's outrage.

Several investigations were conducted—two by the military and another by the Joint Congressional Committee on the Conduct of the War. Horrifying testimony was given by two officers who had refused to obey Chivington's order to attack the sleeping village and had ordered their men to hold their fire. They testified that the Volunteers had committed "the most fearful atrocities that were ever heard of." The Joint Congressional Committee on the War concluded that Chivington "deliberately planned and executed a foul and dastardly massacre....The truth is that he surprised and murdered, in cold blood, the unsuspecting men, women, and children on Sand Creek, who had every reason to believe they were under the protection of the United States authorities."

Chivington was court-martialed for his leadership of the massacre and forced to resign from the militia. An army judge publicly stated that Sand Creek was "a cowardly and a cold-blooded slaughter, sufficient to cover its perpetrators with indelible infamy, and the face of every American with shame and indignation." Governor Evans tried to cover up his part in the massacre, but he was blamed for creating a climate that made it possible. He was forced to resign as governor of the territory, ending his political career and hopes of being elected to the U.S. Senate when Colorado became a state. The 1864 Sand Creek Massacre had a negative effect on the territory's image, and statehood was not approved for 12 more years. It ignited the Colorado War, which expanded into the Plains Wars with the Native Americans, which lasted five times longer than the Civil War, cost thousands of lives, and didn't end until the infamous massacre at Wounded Knee in 1890. Historians identify the Sand Creek Massacre as one of the worst atrocities U.S. citizens ever perpetrated on Native Americans.

The treachery of the Sand Creek Massacre united Indian tribes who'd been enemies for generations. Furious over the deliberate attack on peace-seeking Cheyenne, they laid aside their differences to avenge the massacre and stop the invasion of white people. The Dog Soldiers, a militant warrior society of Cheyenne and Lakota Sioux, vowed, "We have raised the battle axe until death!"

The Colorado War of 1864–65 pitted the Southern Cheyenne, Arapaho, and Lakota Sioux against the U.S. Army, the Colorado militia, and white settlers in the Colorado Territory, western Kansas, and southern Wyoming. Before the end of January 1865, attacks on settlers and travelers on the Colorado plains had increased dramatically. Men, women, and children were killed, scalped, and their bodies mutilated, their wagons and carts plundered, their horses and livestock stolen, their homesteads and cabins burned.

On January 5, 1865, a wagon train heading west on the Overland Trail through northeastern Colorado was attacked by a large Cheyenne war party that killed and scalped 14 men.

On January 7, 1865, about a dozen Cheyenne warriors led by Chief Big Crow attacked Fort Rankin and then turned and fled. The fort commander, Captain O'Brien, and 60 cavalrymen chased them for a few miles, until they reached an area of high bluffs where they were ambushed by more than 1,000 braves. The soldiers whirled about and made a mad dash toward the fort, but 14 cavalrymen and 4 civilians were quickly cut off and killed. Captain O'Brien and the others reached the safety of the fort.

Next, the huge war party galloped up the Platte River and attacked the undefended settlement of Julesburg, an important stage and Pony Express station on the Overland Trail. The 50 men who ran the express office, stables, and stage station escaped to Fort Rankin just before the Indians attacked. The warriors ransacked the express and telegraph offices, tore up the stage

The westward movement of immigrants across the Great Plains caused the Indian Wars—decades of conflict from the 1860s to 1890. *Courtesy of Fine Art of America reproduction of oil painting* Battle at Beecher Island *by Frederic Remington.*

line's headquarters, raided the large supply store and warehouse, rounded up the horses, and carried off all the food and goods.

On January 14, 1865, in northeastern Colorado, two cowboys from the American Ranch were cutting wood when a large war party of Cheyenne and Sioux, hidden in a ravine, suddenly attacked them. The cowboys dived behind their wood pile, and in the skirmish that followed, one man, Big Steve was killed, and the other, Gus Hall, was shot in the ankle. Unable to run, he managed to crawl to a nearby sand bluff, which offered some protection. Hall was trapped there by several warriors, who repeatedly tried to creep up on him. The other Indians rode on toward the American Ranch, where owner Bill Morris and three ranch hands were at work. They killed all four men and then chased down two more cowboys herding cattle and murdered them. They set the ranch house, barn, and outbuildings on fire and captured Sarah Morris as she tried to flee with her two little boys.

The warriors who'd cornered Hall finally abandoned him and rejoined the others and moved on to raid more homesteads. Hall saw the smoke from the burning American Ranch buildings and managed to crawl and walk 12 miles in the frigid night to reach safety at the Wisconsin Ranch.

On January 15, 1865, a large band of Cheyenne and Lakota Sioux attacked Holon Godfrey's isolated ranch northeast of Denver on the Overland Trail. In 1862, Godfrey and his wife, Matilda, opened a small general store and rest

Homesteaders on the plains of Kansas and Colorado were often killed and their cabins destroyed by Cheyenne, Arapaho, and Sioux. *Courtesy of Tom Williams.*

stop on this main route through the Colorado Territory. They sold whiskey, food, and goods and occasionally provided lodging.

Godfrey was prepared for an Indian attack with fortifications to protect his family and property. He'd constructed a six-foot-high adobe wall with strategically placed gun ports around his sod ranch house, stable, and corral. He'd even built a lookout tower, which afforded a view for miles around of the rolling prairie and the Platte River. Godfrey had an impressive stockpile of weapons and ammunition, and he'd even set up a bucket brigade in case the Indians tried to set the place on fire. Late on the night of January 15, when about 130 braves attacked, Godfrey and his three ranch hands were ready.

The Cheyenne raced around the adobe wall trying to punch holes through it, but they were driven off by the defenders' rifle fire from the gun ports. Godfrey's wife and the other women kept the guns reloaded and, when they ran low on ammunition, melted lead bars and quickly made more bullets. The Indians finally managed to break through the end of the wall near the corral and ran off all the horses. Then they shot flaming arrows onto the roof and set the house on fire, so Godfrey's seven children filled buckets of water for a bucket brigade to extinguish the blaze. When the rancher was on the roof fighting the fire, he was suddenly attacked by a warrior who'd gotten inside the yard and climbed up the ladder, knife in hand. Godfrey managed to get off a quick shot, killing his assailant, and went right back to fighting the fire. The rancher knew his small group of defenders would need help if the war party kept up the attack. He was grateful when a ranch hand named Perkins volunteered to try to get through the Indians and go for reinforcements. Late that night, he quietly slipped out of the fortress, crept past the scattered warriors, and reached the Overland Trail. He followed it several miles to the next stage station, where he sent a telegram to Denver, asking for immediate help.

On the following day, January 16, the Indians set fire to the dry grass outside of Godfrey's fortress, which started blazes in the barn and outbuildings. These burning structures were a real danger to the nearby house, so another bucket brigade sent relays of men dashing outside between attacks by the Cheyenne. The defenders finally managed to put the fires out, but the Indians kept up their merciless attack the entire day. Then they set up camp within sight of the fortress but out of rifle range.

On the morning of January 17, the Cheyenne and Sioux resumed the attack but quickly galloped off as a large dust cloud appeared on the western horizon. The exhausted defenders were relieved to see it, and they cheered as a cavalry troop from Fort Morgan rode up to Godfrey's ranch. Days later, Godfrey put up a sign announcing the new name of his ranch, "Fort Wicked." It was unsuccessfully attacked again by the Cheyenne in 1867. In 1869, the Union Pacific Railroad reached Cheyenne, Wyoming, decreasing travel on the Overland Trail and slowing Godfrey's business. Weary of fighting Indians, the tough rancher closed Fort Wicked and moved to Greeley.

On February 2, 1865, Cheyenne, Sioux, and Arapaho warriors raided the stage station at Julesburg again, took all the supplies, and burned the buildings. Once again, Fort Rankin's commander, Captain O'Brien, and 14 troopers made a lucky escape. They were returning to the fort and, at first, were hidden by the smoke from the fires at Julesburg. When the warriors saw them, they quickly attacked, but they were scattered by a round from a howitzer fired from the fort.

The successful attacks on Julesburg were followed by numerous raids up and down the South Platte Trail to Denver and along the Overland Trail to Fort Collins. For six days, smaller war parties from this large body of Cheyenne and Sioux attacked stage stations and homesteads along the Overland Trail. They killed settlers and burned ranches, homesteads, and wagon trains. They stole horses and more than 2,000 cattle. At night, the entire South Platte River Valley was lit up by the flames of fires that were burning homes, barns, outbuilding, everything as the white settlers paid for Chivington's murderous deeds.

On February 4, 1865, more than 100 Cheyenne, Arapaho, and Sioux attacked the Mud Springs stage station in Nebraska. When a troop of 36 cavalrymen arrived, they were surprised by more than 1,000 warriors, who killed one trooper and wounded several others but were finally driven off by fire from the army's howitzer.

On February 6, 1865, 185 cavalrymen came upon a huge force of 5,000 Indians near Rush Creek, Nebraska. The troopers held off the attack with their howitzer, but they were pinned down for four days, until the Indians decided to abandon the fight and continue their journey north to the Powder River Basin of Wyoming. Other smaller groups left the band and went east to join the Northern Cheyenne and Sioux in the Black Hills. This huge body of united tribes had killed more white people than the total number of Cheyenne who'd been massacred at Sand Creek. They'd also destroyed stage stations, killed employees, and stolen the stock across more than 100 miles of the Overland Stage Line through Colorado.

The tribes went into their winter camps, and there was no more trouble until the summer of 1865, when they resumed their daily raids on homesteads, army outposts, and stage stations across Wyoming and Montana. By July, the military had stopped all civilian and commercial travel on the Oregon Trail. The Overland Stage Line couldn't operate because it still didn't have enough horses, and no one wanted the dangerous job of driving a stage or manning a remote station. There was no commercial travel on the Santa Fe Trail through southern Colorado because there were so many Indian attacks. Like a prairie fire, the Colorado War with the Indians had quickly spread north and east across the plains, taking a huge toll on lives and property, hampering western expansion, and slowing the nation's growth.

Congress appropriated barely enough cash to build additional forts, but the demobilized army didn't have enough soldiers to man these scattered posts when they were finally completed. The Union Pacific stopped construction of the transcontinental railroad because so many of its employees had been killed. The number of settlers murdered and homesteads destroyed by Native Americans was growing daily, and there just weren't enough troops in the West to fight the war parties and protect settlers and travelers.

## 2

# SLAVES BECOME SOLDIERS

Private William Cathy, a formerly enslaved man, was tramping through a New Mexican winter night with other soldiers of Company A of the Thirty-Eighth Infantry. These troopers were looking for a camp of Chiricahua Apaches who'd been raiding ranches near Fort Cummings. The men, most of whom were from the Deep South, shivered as a frigid wind blew through their thin uniforms. Their light coats provided little warmth against the cold desert night, and their boots were in tatters from stumbling over miles of rugged, rocky terrain. Two feet of new snow increased their misery and obscured the Apaches' trail, which they'd been following for 17 miserable days in freezing weather. Private Cathy and the men of Company A gratefully turned back toward Fort Cummings.

Private Cathy had enlisted in 1866 in St. Louis with several other men, all formerly enslaved people who were eager for a chance at a new life. He passed a cursory physical exam, was assigned to the Thirty-Eighth Infantry, and was soon marching with other recruits across Kansas to the New Mexico Territory. He'd served two years there when he became desperately ill with smallpox, and his gender was finally discovered. William Cathy was a woman!

A former slave, Cathy Williams had served as a laundress with a Union regiment during the Civil War. After being freed, she decided that the army offered an opportunity, so she changed her name and enlisted. She had no problems as an infantryman until she became ill, and her secret was revealed. Williams was discharged in 1868, the only documented Black woman to enlist as a man and serve as a Buffalo Soldier in the United States Army.

United States Colored Troops veterans who fought in the Civil War were the first to enlist in the Black regiments in 1866. *Courtesy of National Museum of African American History.*

Many USCT veterans who'd fought in the Civil War were so eager to enlist in a Black regiment that they skillfully concealed their injuries or disabilities and slipped by the recruiters. There was no standard physical examination, and since there was a shortage of physicians to screen these recruits, their ailments and physical conditions were often missed, overlooked, or ignored by the harried doctors.

Grizzled men, well past the half-century mark and toughened by a life in the fields, stood quietly in the recruiter's line, hoping for a chance to enlist. Slavery and years of hard work had left their marks; poor nutrition or simply a lack of food, untreated chronic illnesses, and injuries took their toll. Recruiting officers, anxious to fill their quotas, turned away men who were anxious to fight, but whose gnarled hands were too deformed to pull the trigger. They were too lame or bent by arthritis to climb aboard a horse, and their eyesight was so poor that they'd never be able to shoot well. Some were so dull mentally that they could not perform simple tasks without close supervision. The army needed fighting troops, not battalions of laborers, so many thousands of unfit applicants were rejected.

Many formerly enslaved people who tried to enlist were too young to have served in the Civil War; others were far too old. Some recruits, as young as 14 and skilled at lying, successfully passed a cursory physical. These boys gleefully concealed their age because they'd "much ruther be a soljur" or "see the West and fight Injuns!"

# THE RECRUITS

Sergeant Samuel Harris wanted to see the West and believed that his military service would eventually help him get a good government job.

Mazique Santo was interested in getting an education and said, "I felt I wasn't learning enough so I joined."

George Conrad joined the army later, in 1883, and recalled, "I did not learn to read or write until I joined the army."

Private Charles Creek recalled, "I thought there must be a better livin' in this world. I got tired of looking mules in the face sunrise to sunset."

Emmanuel Stance was 19 and barely five feet tall when he enlisted in the Ninth Cavalry in 1866. Stance became the first Buffalo Soldier to be awarded the Medal of Honor, this country's highest military honor.

Stephen Starr was born in Mexico to Mexican and African parents. He came to the United States in 1863 and enlisted in the USCT. He was one of the first to join the new Forty-First Infantry.

Buffalo Soldier, Twenty-Fifth Infantry. Most recruits were illiterate, formerly enslaved people who saw a future in the army. *Courtesy of National Museum of African American History.*

Caleb Benson, orphaned at 14 and unsure of his future as a newly freed teenager, joined the Ninth Cavalry when he was 15, and by age 16, he was battling Apaches in New Mexico.

## ILLITERACY AMONG RECRUITS

There was one common issue among the recruits: when they were asked, "Can you read? Can you write?" The answer was, "No sir, never had no schoolin." The new regiments were filled with 800 to 1,000 recruits each, the majority of whom had no education. Throughout the South, most enslaved people were illiterate because state laws had forbidden teaching them, and the slaveholders risked punishment if they taught them to read and write. Some defied the law and taught their slaves out of a sense of duty or because they felt the state had no right to tell them what to do with their "property." If a company was fortunate enough to sign up a recruit who could read or write, he was usually appointed as quartermaster sergeant with responsibility for maintaining supplies and controlling their use. New recruits with minimal literacy served as noncommissioned officers and clerks and handled muster rolls, supply requisitions, and regimental records. The height requirement of five feet, four inches for any recruit who could read or write was waived, but it didn't solve the problem.

Recognizing the need, Congress authorized a chaplain for each regiment, who would develop an educational curriculum and establish a post school where soldiers would learn to read and write. The new recruits were accustomed to discipline because they'd lived with it their entire lives, and they could be taught to march and drill, to ride and shoot, but they needed a basic education. An army can't always function on direct verbal orders, and soldiers must be able to read written words. Many officers insisted that at least one noncommissioned officer learn to write and read so he could complete supply orders and maintain the unit's records. The regimental chaplains spent as much time teaching the ABCs to Black soldiers, who were eager to learn, as they did holding religious services.

All recruiters made a special effort to recruit blacksmiths, farriers, and saddle-makers for cavalry units, while bakers were needed because the soldiers' diet in the field consisted of bread, bacon, and beans. Colonel Grierson, commander of the Tenth Cavalry, wanted recruiters to make a special effort to sign up musicians for the Regimental Band. Grierson, who was a music teacher before serving in the Civil War, knew the importance of music in brightening the days of his men. He even tried to recruit all the members of a small local band and was disappointed when they didn't want to become soldiers. Men who could not read text or music but had natural musical ability were recruited, and the colonel even taught some music classes to his new band members. Colonel Mackenzie, commander of the Forty-First Regiment, also appreciated the positive effects a military band had on the soldiers' morale and urged recruiters to enlist every musician they found, regardless of his literacy.

The recruiters moved quickly through small towns and rural areas, and training began before the ranks of the Thirty-Eighth Infantry and Tenth Cavalry Regiments were filled. Once the new recruits were signed up, they boarded the Union Pacific train headed west to Fort Leavenworth, Kansas, where cavalry training was underway. The fledgling Ninth Cavalrymen went south to New Orleans, where there was a shortage of officers to train the recruits.

When Congress authorized the new regiments of Black troops, it decided that commanding officers would be white. A board was established to find officer applicants who were not prejudiced against Black soldiers, and a promotion was offered for accepting a command with a Black unit. Since

*Left*: Buffalo Soldier, Twenty-Fifth Infantry Company A in Dakota Territory. Troops moved mail across the territory before the railroad was built. *Courtesy of National Archives.*

*Right*: Reuben Waller, Civil War veteran and original member of the Tenth Cavalry, was with Colonel Carpenter's rescue party at Beecher Island in September 1869. *Courtesy of Anthony Powell.*

recruitment of white officers was slow, Black noncommissioned officers, usually veterans of the USCT, taught the ignorant but willing young recruits how to march and drill. Colonel Hatch, commander of the Ninth Cavalry, managed to recruit eleven officers, most of whom were volunteers who'd signed on to help train the troops and get them up to standard.

# TRAINING OF RECRUITS

Black men who'd spent years behind a mule plowing fields or who'd handled wagon teams and buggies were welcomed by recruiters. There was plenty for them to do in the army: drive supply wagons and ambulances, pack mules and manage pack trains, run stables, and see that the animals were well cared for.

The survival of both young recruits and experienced veterans, who were new to the West and unfamiliar with Indian warfare, depended on their ability to learn quickly. While a soldier's courage, wits, stamina, and endurance were vital for his survival, he needed cooperation between his officers, noncoms, and fellow enlisted men. Cavalrymen and infantrymen learned basic war skills, marksmanship, weapon maintenance, military discipline, physical fitness, survival skills, drills, and marching. Despite the government restrictions on ammunition that limited the amount available for target practice, many recruits became crack shots. They got plenty of exercise on long marches carrying heavy packs and were soon able to walk long distances.

Cavalry recruits learned to ride and to care for their mounts, and they were taught that their lives could depend on their horses. Frontier service was hard on horses that traveled over miles of rough terrain, often at high speeds, lived on weeds and brush without enough water, and were exposed to freezing weather and blistering heat. Hard use, poor forage, dilapidated stables, shortage of veterinarians, and the mistakes made by beginning riders took a heavy toll on these animals. Horses were often deliberately wounded or killed by attacking Indians to eliminate the troopers' means of escape. Thousands of horses were lost during the Indian Wars, and keeping a cavalry regiment mounted was a constant problem for commanders.

A cavalryman carried a single-shot, breech-loading .45-caliber Springfield rifle slung across his shoulder with a revolver, sheath knife, canteen, and at least one hundred pounds of ammunition attached to his "prairie belt." He rode in an uncomfortable McClellan saddle, which was poorly designed with a high cantle front and back and an open two-inch slot in the seat. The men referred to this leather torture chamber as a "ball-crusher." Personal items, gloves, and turpentine for cleaning weapons were carried in a saddlebag. The standard army uniform was blue wool with gold braided piping, and a trooper was occasionally burdened with a cumbersome saber.

When they were in the field, cavalrymen preferred to wear comfortable canvas pants with a buckskin-reinforced seat, crotch, and legs, which they tucked into the tops of their high, leather riding boots. A loose cotton shirt was favored over the traditional five-button tunic. Soldiers usually replaced the hot, felt forage hats with a variety of wide-brimmed cotton or straw hats of their own choice. A wool blanket was carried on the front of the saddle with a coat and rain gear behind. Rank was difficult to distinguish, unless the men were riding in a column, and officers only occasionally wore shoulder patches designating rank.

An infantryman on foot was burdened with a rifle, a pistol, a canteen, ammunition, and the regulation backpack containing a spare uniform, socks, underwear, a tin cup and plate, a sewing kit, and rations rolled up in a blanket. They often marched over rugged terrain under a blistering sun, their boots in tatters, or through howling blizzards with frostbitten toes and fingers.

When they were on scouting expeditions on the Great Plains, troops carried supplies, rations, ammunition, and supplemental feed for the animals in mule-drawn wagons or long pack trains. The army's large, slow-moving columns of men could be easily picked off by Indian marksmen, or they could simply be overrun by attacking war parties. Often, there was little water in the West's dried-up streams and waterholes, and there was only sparse forage for the horses. If a cavalry troop was outfitted with supplies for four days of scouting, any more time spent in this harsh environment worked against them. After days of hard riding over difficult terrain, their animals were usually in poor condition. Weakened horses without water and exhausted, hungry troops on half-rations did not fare well against the overwhelming war parties.

# DUTIES OF TROOPERS

The troopers were spread thinly among the posts scattered around the frontier, and there were not enough men to handle the multitude of tasks. There are few regimental records of the Twenty-Fourth and Twenty-Fifth Infantries, but those soldiers served alongside the cavalrymen across the West. They built roads and bridges and strung miles of telegraph lines, and when there was no infantry at a post, the cavalrymen handled these jobs and fought Indians, too. The infantry troopers learned to ride and often escorted the army paymaster and wagon trains of supplies. They guarded stagecoaches carrying passengers and the mail and patrolled the stage stations and water holes that were vital to roaming Indians. Working with the cavalry, the infantry protected railroad crews and travelers from raiding war parties and bandits and tracked down outlaws and horse thieves.

Garrison duty included logging, operating the fort sawmill if there was one, and making adobe bricks to restore dilapidated buildings. Few soldiers had worked as carpenters, stonemasons, painters, brickmakers, or mechanics, so all work on the deteriorated forts was done by former field hands, cooks, or farmers. These untrained Black troops built Fort Sill and numerous other posts without any expert direction.

Garrison duty also included work in the post garden, which provided fresh green, leafy vegetables to supplement the soldiers' diet of hash, beans and bacon, beef, a mixture called slumgullion stew, hard tack, coffee, molasses and cornbread if they were lucky, and occasionally sweet potatoes. During the 1860s, the army had learned that if soldiers didn't eat vegetables, fruit, or citrus, many developed scurvy.

To prevent scurvy in soldiers before the Civil War, the army created "desiccated vegetables," a mixture of carrots, beets, green beans, turnips, and onions compressed into one-inch by one-foot rectangular bricks. A brick was cooked for hours into a dreadful-tasting stew that made so many sick that the soldiers refused to eat it. Now there were post gardens on the frontier, where soldiers planted seeds, dug irrigation ditches, pulled weeds, and carried buckets of water to fragile plants struggling to survive in arid soil. Harvesting the crops of vegetables, no matter how small, was cause for celebration at the posts, and the mess hall tables were loaded with fresh produce.

Troopers were in the field so much that there was little time to build new barracks, plant gardens, or hunt for game. Classes had to be attended, uniforms mended, boots and weapons cleaned, wood cut, and latrines dug, and building repairs were always waiting. There wasn't much opportunity for recreation for the troops, but gambling and cards were favorite pastimes around the campfire or in the barracks. Occasional horseback riding had to be restricted to the area around the post for safety, and troopers practiced shooting and went hunting when there was time. Many officers believed hunting was an important training method, which increased the soldiers' knowledge of the local area and improved their observation skills, confidence, self-reliance, and marksmanship. Most of the men smoked, drank beer, and sang, and some played the harmonica or banjo.

In the 1860s, the army posts were usually in remote locations where there was little opportunity for soldiers to get in trouble. In the West, the endless plains stretched as far as one could see, and loneliness was a constant companion. Many young recruits, familiar with the green landscape of the South, bursting with trees, plants, and flowers, were stunned by the stark landscape surrounding them. Others, accustomed to the noise and bustle of the northern cities, found the quiet oppressive. The empty horizons were only rarely broken by a solitary figure on horseback or a fast-moving band of shadows, which a soldier could only hope weren't Native Americans. Then the silence would suddenly be splintered by war cries, the buzz of bullets and arrows whistling through the air, cries of pain, and groans of the dying. Life on the plains of Colorado and Kansas for the new recruit was an endless challenge of grim reality.

There was little to relieve the daily monotony, loneliness, and boredom of garrison life. Music was a positive diversion for the soldiers, and Colonel Grierson of the Tenth Cavalry recognized the benefits that came from building a Regimental Band. Even if a man could not play an instrument but had an obvious musical inclination, he could earn a place in the band. Since the regiment had no instruments, and there was no money to buy any, Grierson established a band fund, and all of the enlisted men were asked to contribute fifty cents apiece every month. Each group of company officers donated fifty dollars monthly to the band fund.

The soldiers of the Tenth Cavalry took great pride in their band, which played at special events and parties on the post, led military parades, and performed for Fourth of July celebrations. The Regimental Band added flavor and color to ceremonies, and band members got a welcome break from garrison life when they traveled off-post for events. As settlements developed near posts, the band was invited to perform for special occasions, local parades, and political rallies, and often gave Sunday afternoon concerts. Smaller groups of musicians played for weddings, dances, and community activities.

Married or single, a soldier's life in a remote outpost was often lonely and full of longing for the companionship of friends and relatives back home. White officers were allowed to have their families with them at most frontier posts, and a certain amount of housing was available for them. The new posts that were built in the 1870s had even more family housing for officers, but there were often vacancies. Many military wives didn't like the harsh environment and isolation of frontier posts and preferred to remain in the comfort of their homes in the East.

During the 1860s, most of the young enlisted men in the Black regiments were single, but by the 1870s, many had married after deciding on a military career. During this time, a married Black man could not bring his family to the post, creating a hardship. Military leaves were not granted routinely, and if a soldier had not been home during his five years on the frontier, he was often reluctant to reenlist due to this harsh policy.

This policy changed in the late 1870s, when the families of enlisted men were welcome at frontier posts. However, the army provided housing on the post for families of white officers only, which left the enlisted men on their own to find a place to live with their wives and children. Often, there was no rental housing off-post, so some families were forced to live in sheds and dilapidated shacks. Fort Robinson's surgeon, Jefferson Kean, reported on the living conditions of a Black corporal, his wife, and their child. Unable to rent even a tiny cabin, they were living in a one-room shack, which the physician said was "made of scrap lumber, about 12 feet square with one door and no window." He continued, "The door provided the only ventilation, and admitted light and dust in equal quantities."

Despite these difficulties, most married Black soldiers tried to bring their families west. The 1893 census at Fort Robinson reported 14 white soldier families and 25 Black families living there. The wives of Black enlisted men often worked as post laundresses, cooks, or maids.

Families of enlisted men weren't welcome at forts, until the 1870s. These families at Fort Garland, Colorado, welcomed enlisted men home after months on patrol. *Courtesy of History Colorado.*

Conditions at most frontier posts were primitive, and several cholera epidemics swept through, killing many soldiers. It was years before army doctors learned that cholera was caused by contaminated drinking water and realized the importance of adequate sewage management and disinfection, and took aggressive action to stop the spread of disease among the soldiers.

In addition to cholera, there were other problems, like the rabid wolf that invaded the post hospital at Fort Larned, Kansas. With one bite, the large gray creature snapped off the finger of a corporal who was trying to chase him out of the building. Then the crazed animal attacked another soldier who was trying to run away and sank his fangs into the man's foot and clamped down. Screaming wildly, the frantic man hit the wolf repeatedly with a chair and finally freed his badly chewed foot. Then the wild-eyed wolf, jaws dripping and foaming, raced around the hospital ward snapping at anything that moved. Drawn by the ruckus, a guard rushed in and took aim at the animal, but in the excitement, he missed his target, and the wolf escaped, dashing right between his legs. The wolf loped across the parade ground to the officers' quarters, where he darted in an open door and created more chaos, snapping and snarling as everyone scattered in fear. Then the wolf bit a lieutenant in the leg before racing off to hide in a haystack in the adjoining field. Troopers followed him there, and a lucky shot ended the creature's dangerous rampage. At this time, Louis Pasteur was working on a treatment for humans who'd been bitten by rabid animals, but it was still in the development stage. Unfortunately, the *Medical History of Fort Larned* does not report the treatment of these soldiers' bites or the outcome of their cases

# 3

# THE TENTH CAVALRY

## *"Ready and Forward"*

When the Civil War began, Benjamin Grierson quit his job as a music teacher to enlist in the Union army. He volunteered for the infantry because he was skittish around horses after being kicked in the face when he was eight years old. His bushy black beard concealed the large scar on his face that resulted from the injury. Despite his lack of military experience and distrust of horses, Grierson found himself a Union major in charge of a cavalry unit, the Sixth Illinois. He led a 600-mile dash through Mississippi, burning Confederate supply stations, tearing up railroad tracks, and cutting a ruinous swath through the South. General Grant credited Grierson's Raid for its important role in the fall of Vicksburg and promoted him to colonel.

After the Civil War, Grierson became commander of the Tenth Cavalry. He often said Black men were brave soldiers, worthy of respect, who would provide military service that was "full of honor and gallantry." Recruitment for the regiment was slow because Grierson insisted that recruiters sign up "superior men," and that "quality is more important than numbers." As a result, only 392 men had enlisted by May 1867, but recruiters continued to work, and within a few months, 702 new soldiers had reported to Fort Leavenworth for training. The recruits adopted the motto "Ready and Forward" for the Tenth Regiment. Since there were only a few white officers, the experienced Black noncommissioned officers took charge of the training. Many USCT veterans knew how to use a rifle and revolver, but they did not know how to ride or care for their horses.

William Hoffman, the commander of Leavenworth, made living conditions for the new Black recruits as uncomfortable as possible. They were housed in the fort's old barracks on land that became a swamp every time it rained. Many developed pneumonia, and others suffered from a cholera outbreak. Hoffman refused Grierson's requests for different quarters for his men and even ignored his request to put in wooden walkways over the mud. The commander denied Grierson's requests for equipment and wouldn't allow the Black troops to practice their drills or use the fort's parade grounds. Hoffman bombarded Grierson with petty, false charges against individual Black soldiers and even ordered him to keep his men at least 15 feet away from the white troops.

Despite cholera and pneumonia, Colonel Grierson had eight companies trained and ready for the field by August 1867, when they were transferred to Fort Riley, Kansas. One of their most important jobs was protecting the work crews that were building the transcontinental railroad. Determined to stop the railroad, Indians continued their attacks on work crews in 1867. They tore up newly laid tracks, and knocked down telegraph lines as fast as they were erected. War parties rampaged over the plains of western Kansas and eastern Colorado. They stopped the stage lines, disrupted mail service

The Tenth Cavalry at Fort Apache, Arizona, in 1887 wore leftover Civil War white gloves at dress parade, despite austere conditions at southwestern posts. *Courtesy of University of Arizona Library.*

and travel to Denver, California, and Oregon. The stages often carried soldiers for protection, but the attacks continued. Only two stagecoaches reached Denver in six months, leaving its citizens without mail or any communication from the East.

The new troopers of the Tenth Cavalry accompanied stages and wagon trains from Fort Wallace near the Colorado border and along the dangerous Smoky Hill Trail to Denver. The Cheyenne Dog Soldiers lurked around Fort Wallace and often waylaid wood cutters and small groups of troops that left the safety of the post. As they grew bolder, large Cheyenne war parties repeatedly attacked Fort Wallace itself.

Three companies of the Tenth Regiment were sent to Texas to join the Ninth in its endless battles with the Kiowa and Comanche. As the Union Pacific Railroad moved west across Kansas, nine companies of the Tenth Cavalry were stationed at Forts Hays, Harker, and Larned to guard the railroad crews and patrol for war parties around the Solomon, Saline, and Arkansas Rivers.

# HANCOCK'S WAR

In 1867, General Winfield Scott Hancock was commander of the Department of the Missouri, which included Missouri, Kansas, Colorado, and New Mexico Territory, where Native Americans were taking bloody revenge for the Sand Creek Massacre. Hancock came west with little knowledge or understanding of the Plains Indians, but he was quite confident that he could bring them under control. He met with several Cheyenne chiefs at Fort Larned, Kansas, in April 1867 and then made plans to meet other leaders in their village at Pawnee Forks to discuss peace.

General Hancock was accompanied by a large number of troops, terrifying the Cheyenne survivors of Sand Creek who lived in the village. These women and children fled, leaving their tipis and belongings behind. Instead of trying to understand their fear, Hancock was offended, viewing this as a personal insult, and demanded that they return or he would not hold peace talks. Some chiefs, hoping to appease him, rode out to find their families but returned alone. As Hancock fumed, the others quietly drifted away, hoping to avoid more trouble.

In a fit of temper, Hancock ordered the troops to burn the village and destroy the Indians' food and supplies. He justified this in his report to the

War Department, saying, "I am satisfied that this Indian village was a nest of conspirators." As word of the destruction at Pawnee Forks spread, the angry Native Americans increased their attacks on settlers, wagon trains, and railroad crews across Kansas and Colorado. Travel on the Santa Fe and Overland Trails was disrupted, and large war parties clustered around Forts Hays and Harker, killing anyone who approached, and running off the nearby stage station's horses. Four men were killed and scalped near Fort Wallace, and two teamsters hauling rock from a local quarry were killed and scalped within sight of that post.

The Tenth Cavalry spent this summer of escalating violence, called Hancock's War, scouring the plains of Colorado and western Kansas for Indians in the valleys around the Republican and Smoky Hill Rivers. Patrolling with the Eighteenth Kansas Volunteers, the inexperienced troopers had several skirmishes with war parties on four different streams in Kansas, all of them named Beaver Creek. On June 21, 1867, the Pond Creek station of the Butterfield Overland stage line near the Colorado-Kansas border was attacked by a war party of Cheyenne and Lakota Sioux. The Indians were finally driven off by the desperate efforts of a company of Seventh Cavalry, but they returned several more times, attacking this station until all stage service was halted.

On June 21, Black troopers of the Thirty-Eighth Regiment were on picket duty near Fort Wallace when it was attacked by war chief, Roman Nose, with a large band of Cheyenne. This garrison was still under construction and didn't have a protective outer wall. Seeing that the defending troops were outnumbered and desperately needed help, the Black soldiers jumped into a wagon pulled by a mule team and raced toward the defenders' skirmish line. The driver lashed the mules with his long bullwhip, shouting at them as they ran, while the troopers, standing in the wagon, kept up steady gunfire at the Cheyenne. When they reached the fort, they jumped out of the wagon, joined the defenders, and continued shooting until the Cheyenne finally withdrew. There was a lot of congratulatory backslapping as everyone praised the men of the Thirty-Eighth for driving off the attackers.

The following day, a large wagon train led by Francisco Baca was attacked by 75 Cheyenne near Cimarron Crossing on the Santa Fe Trail. Historic accounts vary about the number of casualties, but these frequent attacks slowed commercial travel on the trail and significantly increased the fear of the settlers.

On June 26, 1867, Corporal Turner and 11 troopers of K Company were guarding a survey party at Wilson's Creek, about 30 miles west of Fort Harker.

Early that morning, they were attacked by Indians who shot into their tents, but luckily, no soldiers were hit. Scrambling about, Corporal Turner and his men made good use of the 50 rounds of ammunition they carried and repulsed the Indians, killing 5 warriors and several of their ponies.

That same day, June 26, 1867, Fort Wallace was again attacked, but the Indians were driven back. Then a railroad survey party, escorted by the Seventh Cavalry, was attacked by several hundred warriors near Beaver Creek. Sergeant Frederick Wyllyams, who'd joined the army after emigrating from Great Britain, was killed. After about three hours of fierce fighting, the Indians retreated, and the troops raced back to Fort Wallace.

When the troops returned later to retrieve Wyllyams's body, they found his naked, scalped corpse had been horribly mutilated. A photograph of this gruesome sight was taken by Wyllyams's friend and fellow Briton, William Bell, the survey party's photographer. This grisly photograph appeared in a national publication, horrifying the country and increasing anger against Native Americans. The image of this soldier's ghastly fate was undoubtedly firmly fixed in the minds of all soldiers. Later that day, the stage station at Black Butte Creek was attacked, but the Indians were driven off.

In early July, young Lieutenant Kidder and a ten-man patrol were dispatched from Fort Sedgwick, Colorado, to deliver a message to Colonel Custer, camped 90 miles east on the Republican River with a Seventh Cavalry company. Kidder couldn't locate Custer, and around July 1, his small party was attacked by a band of Sioux and Cheyenne. The troopers dashed to a ravine for shelter, but they were quickly overrun, and every man was killed.

Over a week later, on July 12, Custer came upon the decomposing bodies of Kidder and his men, some of whom had as many as 20 to 40 arrows sticking in them. They had been scalped and mutilated. The bodies were buried on the site in a common grave but were eventually removed to the cemetery at Fort Leavenworth. Lieutenant Kidder's body was identified by a piece of material from a shirt his mother had made, and his remains were sent home for burial in Minnesota.

A few days later, Corporal Alfred Bradden and 10 Black troopers from the Thirty-Eighth Infantry were escorting a wagon train to Fort Wallace when they were attacked by about 25 Indians. The troopers' rifle fire drove them back, but the wagon train was closely followed to the fort by a war party of more than 300 braves.

Four companies of the Eighteenth Kansas Volunteer Cavalry were based at Fort Hays to serve with 135 Black troopers of the Tenth Cavalry. When a combined group of these troops were scouting along the Saline River in July, they were attacked by 400 Kiowa and Cheyenne led by war chiefs Satanta and Roman Nose. They eventually drove the Indians back to Prairie Dog Creek and then charged a second large war party that had gathered to watch the first fight. This band was caught by surprise, and the troopers' well-placed rifle shots quickly scattered them into a full retreat. There was plenty of laughter and joking among the combined Black and white force of local militia and young troopers on their triumphant ride back to Fort Hays.

On July 21, Sergeant Reid and 10 men of Company C Thirty-Eighth Infantry, who were escorting a wagon train of supplies to a small outpost in western Kansas, stopped for the night. Their camp was attacked around midnight by about 400 Cheyenne Dog Soldiers, who tried to stampede the mule teams and threw torches into the wagons. The troopers dashed about putting out fires, dodging arrows, and trying to shoot their attackers as the teamsters circled the wagons. After about two hours, the Cheyenne suddenly turned around and left, taking their dead and wounded. There were no casualties among the troopers, who quickly loaded up and headed for Fort Hays, reaching it with no further trouble.

This summer of violence continued when the Cheyenne attacked the tiny settlement of Brookville, Kansas, a small branch of the transcontinental railway. They were determined to destroy the railroad shops and roundhouse with the steam engine inside. The railroad men in Brookville had received a warning telegram from the engineer of a train heading east that had seen the large war party approaching the station. The employees quickly gathered their families inside the roundhouse, and when the Indians raced into Brookville, they found no one, so they piled railroad ties against the sides of the roundhouse, intending to burn down the building. The quick-thinking railroad crew fired up the steam engine's boiler, loaded everyone on, and the engineer hit full throttle. The steam engine blasted right through the roundhouse doors, sending railroad ties and Indians flying as it steamed off, headed for safety in Salina.

On August 1, 1867, a band of 80 Cheyenne attacked a camp of railroad workers, killing 7 men. Captain George Armes and Company F of the Tenth Cavalry, with about 100 inexperienced soldiers, a few USCT veterans, and Kansas Volunteers, pursued these Indians up the Saline River until they scattered.

On August 2, 1867, Indians raided the Big Creek stage station and killed one employee, and then they attacked Captain Armes and his men, who were scouting along the Saline River. This band of about 75 Cheyenne Dog

J. C. H. Grabill, Photographer,
Sturgis, Dakota Ter.

Buffalo Soldier. The Cheyenne Indians called men of the Tenth Cavalry "Buffalo Soldiers" because they said their curly hair, dark skin, and courage reminded them of their revered buffalo. *Courtesy of National Archives.*

Soldiers was soon joined by more braves, and when the cavalrymen dismounted to fight, they were quickly surrounded by more than 400 wildly whooping warriors. Most of the Indians were armed with Spencer rifles and revolvers and had plenty of ammunition, but luckily for the troops, they were not good shots. This fight went on for six hours, until the troopers ran low on bullets, and Captain Armes decided they must make a run for it. The men jumped on their horses and shot their way through the surrounding Cheyenne, who chased them for 16 miles before they finally turned back. In this running skirmish, Captain Armes said the Indians fired at least 2,000 shots. Despite their poor marksmanship, the Cheyenne wounded Armes in the hip, and one of the new recruits, Sergeant William Christy, was hit in the head and killed. Christy, a young farmer from Pennsylvania, had been with the regiment less than two months and was the first Tenth Cavalry trooper killed in combat. Captain Armes reported that at least 6 Indians were killed, and several were wounded, saying, "It is the greatest marvel in the world that my command and myself escaped being massacred." Armes, who was never generous with praise, wrote that the inexperienced Black soldiers "fought with courage and perseverance under dangers most trying."

That same day, a group of Eighteenth Kansas Volunteers scouting along the Solomon River north of Fort Riley was attacked by another large war party. After a fierce battle, the Volunteers were able to fight their way back to Fort Hays.

## Buffalo Soldiers Get Their Name

About this time, the Cheyenne gave the men of the Tenth Cavalry their nickname of "Buffalo Soldiers" because they thought their dark, curly hair and dusky skin resembled that of the buffalo. At first, these Indians held the Black soldiers in utter contempt, calling them "white soldiers with black faces," but the soldiers' courage and tough fighting ability, like that of the honored buffalo, earned the warriors' respect. This nickname was given to all Black troops, and the Tenth Cavalry designed the figure of the buffalo into its regimental crest.

On August 19, the Dog Soldiers attacked a party of wood cutters on Twin Butte Creek, killing three men and driving off 25 animals. The following day, they stole a herd of cattle, and on the next, they attacked two stages headed for Cheyenne Wells, Colorado, and chased both back to Fort Wallace. They raided a ranch in western Kansas near Fort Wallace and killed three cowboys. Then the Cheyenne doubled back and attacked the stage station at Pond Creek near Fort Wallace, drove off the horses, and killed both station hands. They headed southwest toward Fort Dodge, killed a herder on the way, and made off with his livestock.

Only 19 days after being wounded in the fight on the Saline River, Captain Armes was back in the saddle, leading a scouting party of 40 Buffalo Soldiers and 90 men of the Eighteenth Kansas Volunteer Cavalry, commanded by Captains Jenness and Baker. They left Fort Hays and headed north toward the headwaters of the Solomon and Republican Rivers and turned toward Beaver Creek. The following evening, Captain Jenness and a detachment of Kansas Volunteers rode out to investigate a light on the eastern prairie. They found a campfire in an abandoned Indian camp, but when they attempted to return to the other troops, they became confused in the darkness and, rather than wandering about on the prairie, camped and waited for daylight.

Saddling up early the next morning, Captain Jenness and his Volunteers located Armes's campsite, but the troops had already moved out, so they followed their trail and caught up with their slow-moving supply train. As these Volunteers neared Prairie Dog Creek, they were suddenly attacked by a large body of Cheyenne. The teamsters quickly pulled their wagons into a protective circle with the horses inside as the Volunteers, armed with Spencer repeating carbines and 200 rounds of ammunition each, managed to hold the Indians at bay. Several howling Dog Soldiers dashed boldly through the wagon circle, trying to frighten the horses by flapping blankets at their heads and waving their lances. The battle raged all day, and when darkness finally came, Captain Jenness and his men left the wagons and quietly retreated, following a buffalo trail back along the Solomon River. They hid in thick willows under the overhanging banks of a deep ravine and quickly threw up a breast works of driftwood and rocks for protection. Unfortunately, the sharp-eyed Indians tracked them to their hiding place and swooped down, attacking with renewed vigor.

Meanwhile, Captain Armes's troops had moved farther up Prairie Dog Creek, and they, too, were being attacked by a war party of about 400 Cheyenne. The well-armed Buffalo Soldiers were greatly outnumbered, but they put up such a heroic defense in the daylong battle that the Indians drifted away at nightfall. Armes posted sentries to keep watch, but there was little sleep that night for anyone.

Dawn brought the Indians roaring back, and Captain Armes decided they had to make a run for it or die right there. The Buffalo Soldiers and Kansas Volunteers mounted the horses that had survived the first attack, and with some riding double, they charged straight through the hordes of howling Cheyenne. Warriors swarmed everywhere, and several troopers were wounded and fell from their horses. Their fellows quickly grabbed them, dragging them up onto their mounts as they raced east, hoping to reach the safety of the fort. As arrows whistled by and bullets whizzed past their heads, the furious warriors closed in.

Suddenly, Armes heard gunfire and the sounds of a battle and turned his troops toward the ravine, where Captain Jenness and the Kansas Volunteers were under attack. The Buffalo Soldiers charged and drove off the smaller war party, but their own pursuers were very close. Jumping into the ravine, they joined Jenness and his men, keeping up the fight all day against the huge war party of very determined Indians. Again and again, daring braves dashed close to the soldiers' lines, screaming insults and taunting them.

In a desperate move, Captain Armes and about 20 troopers suddenly raced out of the ravine and charged up a nearby hill, attacking a large group of warriors waiting there as reserves. Surprised by this sudden move, these Cheyenne scattered and rode off, ending the day's fighting. The cavalry lost 3 men and had 36 wounded, while Armes estimated that 50 Indians were killed and about 150 wounded. The officers believed they had been attacked by at least 800 to 1,000 Indians. Once the Cheyenne withdrew, the soldiers loaded the wounded men on the surviving horses, galloped out of the ravine and rode as fast as possible to the safety of Fort Hays. This Battle of Prairie Dog Creek ended the U.S. offensive operations on the Kansas frontier for 1867, and there was hope that a treaty would soon be developed with the tribes of the Southern Plains.

On September 9, 1867, a small train of seven wagons, a carriage, and an ambulance was headed for Albuquerque through Kansas on the Santa Fe Trail. Despite warnings of war parties in the area, the owner, Franz Huning, was too impatient to wait for a Tenth Cavalry escort and went on alone. The wagon train was attacked, and three people were killed, but Huning and the rest escaped while the Indians were busy plundering the wagons and stealing the mules. Days later, Huning returned to retrieve the three scalped and mutilated bodies of his friends.

On September 15, 1867, Sergeant Charles Davis and eight troopers of the Tenth Cavalry were patrolling the Union Pacific tracks west of Fort Hays. Private John Randall, who'd been with the regiment less than two months, and two railroad employees left the work camp to check another site when a war party of about 70 Cheyenne suddenly swooped down on them. The two railroad employees were killed immediately, and Randall was shot in the hip. He managed to scramble into a hole under the overhanging cut-bank of a nearby stream, but the Indians saw him. They galloped their horses back and forth across Randall's hiding place and caved in large portions of the stream's bank, exposing the trooper. Then they charged forward, throwing their sharp lances at him, while the most daring closed in, jabbing the young trooper with their long, sharp weapons. Randall continued to fight, despite being stabbed 11 times in his shoulders and back. Digging frantically with his bare hands, he managed to burrow farther back into the bank. From his hole, he waited for an eager Cheyenne to peek over the edge of the stream bank and then fired his revolver, making every shot count. Finally, the Indians grew tired of trying to get Randall out of his hole and losing warriors to his accurate aim, so they rode off.

Next, this same band of Indians attacked two men driving an oxen team toward Fort Hays, but when they heard the gunshots, Sergeant Davis and the Buffalo Soldiers quickly responded. They surprised the attackers and managed to hold them off while the team of oxen lumbered to the work crew's camp. When Sergeant Davis noticed that Randall and the two civilian workers were missing, he and seven soldiers began searching for them and were surprised by another large war party hiding in two nearby ravines. Somehow the Buffalo Soldiers' rapid rifle fire and accurate aim created such disorder among the Indians that the troopers succeeded in surrounding the war party, stampeding their horses, and forcing them to flee on foot, leaving 13 dead braves.

Sergeant Davis and his men continued to search for Randall, whose cries for help finally led them to his hiding place. Bleeding profusely and in serious condition, the wounded soldier was extracted from the hole and carried back to camp. The tough trooper's wounds were treated, but it was a while before he rode with the cavalry again. That fall, Private Randall was surprised with a citation for his heroism.

During the remainder of the summer of 1867, the Indian attacks on wagon trains and travelers in Colorado and Kansas continued. Settlers fled their burning homes along the Overland Trail, and the route was closed again because there were so many Indian raids. Large war parties and small bands of Indians roamed the region, attacking settlers along the Platte River in the north and raiding every stage station along the Smoky Hill Trail farther south. There were so many attacks on railroad work crews that all construction on the transcontinental railroad was stopped again. Every stage station 150 miles east of Fort Wallace and 150 miles west into Colorado had been attacked by Indians numerous times, their horses run off, their employees wounded or killed.

Farther south, there were so many attacks on the stage station at the Cimarron Crossing of the Arkansas River on the Santa Fe Trail that it closed, too. Westbound trade wagons loaded with goods were frequently attacked by Indians, their teamsters killed, and the merchandise and animals stolen. Large war parties of Cheyenne, Arapaho, Sioux, Kiowa, and Comanches roamed the southern part of Kansas and Colorado Territories, destroying homesteads and preying on stagecoaches and travelers, despite their military escorts.

On August 25, 1867, Colorado's Governor Hall telegraphed Washington that Indians were devastating southern Colorado and asked for help. During the following days, two settlers were killed near Fort Lyon in southeastern Colorado, and then 30 Indians attacked the stage near Cheyenne Wells, east of Denver on the Smoky Hill Trail. The coach was escorted by a small group of Buffalo Soldiers from Fort Wallace, who galloped alongside and fought off the attackers. The passengers cowered on the floor as the stage swayed and bounced over the trail, and the determined Cheyenne closed in. The troopers dodged their arrows and made every rifle shot count, while the driver urged the team on. The stage and its escort finally managed to outrun the Indians, but they spent the rest of the ride to Denver looking over their shoulders, fearing another attack.

An army wagon train full of supplies for Fort Lyon was attacked by more than 250 Indians on the Santa Fe Trail and forced to return to Fort Dodge. On August 27, Colorado's Governor Hall sent a second telegram to the War Department asking for more help because the Indians were continuing their raids, killing settlers, and destroying ranches. Migrant wagon trains and stages were being attacked, and no one was safe.

# October 1867 Medicine Lodge Treaty

By October 1867, General Hancock had been removed from command and replaced by General Philip Sheridan. Hancock's stubborn pride and ignorance had created havoc on the plains and incited the tribes with his petty decision to burn the village at Pawnee Forks. This had started Hancock's War, a series of conflicts that brought untold misery to Indians and Americans alike, and disrupted U.S. and Indian relations for more than a decade.

In the fall, negotiations were completed between the Indian Peace Commission and the tribes, who were still determined to stop white settlement in Kansas and Colorado. It was estimated that 5,000 to 15,000 Kiowa, Comanche, Southern Cheyenne, Arapaho, and Kiowa-Apaches met with government representatives on Medicine Lodge Creek, Kansas. After a week of tense negotiations, each tribe agreed to go to a reservation but retained their hunting rights in the territory south of the Arkansas River. The government promised to provide them with educational, medical, and agricultural assistance, as well as food, clothing, and other annuities.

Three Medicine Lodge Treaties were developed, each specific to certain tribes. The Indians agreed to keep the peace and promised not to attack settlers or oppose construction of the railroad or military roads. They agreed to stay away from the main travel routes and gave up all claim to lands outside their reservations. The Medicine Lodge Treaties brought a temporary peace to the Plains, although the Cheyenne were unhappy because buffalo were much less plentiful on the barren, dry section of land that was to be their reservation. Many of the chiefs were opposed to the treaty's terms and refused to sign it.

In 1868, Congress didn't ratify the treaties of Medicine Lodge, so once again, money was not appropriated for the supplies and food for the Indians. When rations didn't arrive at the reservations as promised, the situation grew critical in Texas, Kansas, and Colorado. In the early summer, large numbers of Cheyenne showed up at Fort Larned, asking for the goods that were promised in the treaty. Congress continued to delay, and money was not appropriated. The United States had broken the Medicine Lodge Treaties before a year had passed, and the disgusted Indians returned to their barren reservation empty-handed.

During 1868, the Plains tribes kept the terms of the treaty and did not interfere with the railroad construction. Now the Union Pacific chugged safely past Fort Riley, Fort Hays, Fort Wallace, and across the eastern plains of Colorado, reaching Cheyenne, Wyoming, in November 1868.

While Congress haggled and dithered about ratifying the treaties, the Kiowas and Comanches began raiding Texas settlements. Then they attacked the Cherokees and Choctaws, who were among the Five Nations living peacefully in Indian Territory. In late August 1868, Congress finally approved the treaties, but the vital rations and food did not reach the starving tribes for many more months. These delays endangered settlers and travelers, as the Indians were increasingly desperate and angry about the government's broken promises.

# 4

# The Battle of Beecher Island, 1868, and Sheridan's Winter Campaign, 1868–69

In 1868, the Indians began leaving the reservations to hunt for food, and if there were no buffalo around, they stole settlers' cattle. This led to open conflict with ranchers and homesteaders in Kansas and Colorado, and the Tenth Cavalry often tracked down these bands and forced them back to their reservations in Indian Territory.

On August 1, 1868, Captain Graham was leading a Tenth Cavalry company along the Smoky Hill Trail, scouting for Indian raiding parties that had been attacking travelers and stagecoaches. When they neared Big Sandy Creek, they were ambushed by about 100 Cheyenne. It was this company's first battle with Indians, and although greatly outnumbered, the men fought like cornered wildcats, putting their new Spencer repeating rifles to good use and proving the hours of practice were worthwhile. Several Black soldiers were crack shots, and the troopers held off the Indians until the sun went down. As darkness fell, the war party rode off, leaving 11 dead warriors and 14 wounded; the cavalry had 1 man wounded, but 14 horses were killed.

## Battle of Beecher Island

In August 1868, General Sheridan suddenly decided that small groups of well-armed, experienced frontiersmen were more mobile and could track down roving bands of Indians better than military troops. Putting this idea

*Left*: Beecher Island, a lonely place on the northeastern Colorado plains where 50 frontiersmen were under siege by a huge war party of Indians from September 17 to 25, 1868. *Courtesy of Tom Williams.*

*Below*: Some 700 Cheyenne and Sioux warriors attacked Forsyth's scouts at the Arikaree branch of Republican River in Colorado Territory in September 1898 during the Battle of Beecher Island. *Harpers Weekly Illustrated Magazine, 1895.*

into action, he ordered Lieutenant George Forsyth to recruit 50 frontiersmen to scout around the Republican River in western Kansas and into eastern Colorado. The scouts were to track down and eliminate the large Cheyenne war parties raiding in this region.

Forsyth quickly recruited a company of experienced frontiersmen and scouts, most of whom had lost relatives and friends to Indian attacks. They set out from Fort Hays and, near the Colorado border, came on the tracks of a large body of Indians, including women and children. Jack Stillwell, a veteran scout, advised Forsyth that they should turn back because it was obvious that this was an entire village, and their small company was greatly outnumbered. Forsyth shrugged off the advice, replying that they'd come to fight Indians, and that's what they were going to do. The experienced scouts were worried but continued to follow the Indians' tracks up the Arikaree Fork of the Republican River. After dark, they made camp by the shallow Arikaree River, which was nearly dry.

The morning of September 17, 1868, dawned cool and clear, but the early quiet was suddenly shattered as eight screaming warriors dashed over a ridge toward the scouts' tethered horses. "Turn out! Turn out! Indians!" Forsyth yelled as the men grabbed their rifles and dashed for their horses. A huge horde of screaming Indians charged toward them from the southwest, while others swarmed over ridges from the east and west on their fast ponies. It was an appalling sight as at least 700 Cheyenne Dog Soldiers and Sioux, in fierce warpaint and feathered headdresses, waving their lances, raced straight at them.

Forsyth and his men ran to a small island that was scarcely a sandbar in the middle of the Arikaree, secured their horses to willow bushes, and began digging pits in the sand with their tin cups and spoons. There was no shelter, just a few cottonwoods and one dense stand of willows. Some of the men wanted to make a run for it, but Forsyth shouted, "Stay where you are! It's our only chance! I'll shoot down any man who tries to leave!" So, they stayed and burrowed deeper into their sandy pits. The Indians charged straight at them, but the scouts began shooting their repeating Spencer rifles, which could fire seven shots before reloading. Their aim was deadly, and as braves were hit and fell, their oncoming line split, and the thundering horde galloped past on each side of the tiny island. Some of the Indians had rifles that had to be reloaded after each shot, so they couldn't match the deadly volleys fired by the scouts. Forsyth's men were greatly outnumbered, so their only hope was to keep shooting to drive their attackers back. The second wave came quickly, and in minutes, the scouts were surrounded by screaming braves circling the island, round and round. Barrages of arrows made pincushions of the horses and mules, and they dropped screaming in their tracks.

The frontiersmen dodged bullets from Indian snipers, who crept close and hid in the tall grass along the river bank. Then a Cheyenne warrior named Wolf Belly dashed right through their rifle pits, wheeled his horse around, and charged back through the men, emerging unscathed. Wolf

The Arikaree Branch of Republican River is shallow and narrow today, like in 1868. The small sandbar with its lone cottonwood and clump of willows provided little protection. *Courtesy of Tom Williams.*

Belly was a fearful sight, wearing a cougar skin, with feathers woven through his long black hair, his face covered with stripes of red and black, and screaming a fierce war cry. The air was filled with gun smoke, the screams of the wounded men and the dying horses, and the terrifying shrieks of the Indians. Lieutenant Beecher, a nephew of abolitionist Henry Ward Beecher, directed the scouts to pile up the horse carcasses to make protective breastworks. As the Indians crept nearer in a third wave, the scouts rose to fire from their rifle pits, and Forsyth suddenly toppled backward, a bullet in his right thigh. Moments later, a second bullet hissed through the air, striking him in his left leg, shattering the bone. The major was unable to walk and was trying to crawl across the sand when the doctor, who was coming to help him, was shot in the forehead. Next, Lieutenant Beecher was shot. The young officer, his blue jacket soaked with blood, fell back into his rifle pit and died. Forsyth was hit again, but this time a sniper's bullet grazed his head, leaving a bloody groove. An arrow hit scout Frank Harrington in the forehead, and when a friend tried to pull it out, the shaft broke off, leaving the arrowhead protruding. Then another bullet struck Harrington, hitting the arrowhead and sending it flying harmlessly out of his skull!

As their one remaining horse was felled by a bullet, the scouts heard someone among the enemy clearly yell, "There goes the last damn horse anyhow!" Some of the frontiersmen believed this was George Bent, the half-Cheyenne son of William Bent, who'd started the trading post of Bent's Fort. George lived with the Cheyenne and was in the Sand Creek village when it was attacked by Chivington and the Colorado Volunteers. After the 1864 massacre of his Indian relatives and friends, George Bent joined the Cheyenne Dog Soldiers, an elite warrior society, and took part in many attacks against the white people.

Around noon, there was a lull in the fighting as a huge number of Indians gathered on a hill within sight of the pinned-down scouts. Then one of the tallest Indians they'd ever seen rode up, and the scouts knew this was the Cheyenne war leader Roman Nose. Wherever he led the Dog Soldiers, crowds of young braves eagerly followed him. After the Sand Creek Massacre, he'd become a principal figure among his people, leading strikes against settlers in eastern Colorado and in the destruction and burning of Julesburg, Colorado, in 1865. War parties of Dog Soldiers led by Roman Nose pillaged and killed throughout the Powder River country of Wyoming, ranging into Nebraska and down through Kansas. Roman Nose was admired by the other Indians for his daring charges straight into the enemy's face and his bold dashes up and down in front of the troops within easy rifle range, tempting them to waste their ammunition by shooting at him repeatedly. He led countless attacks and always emerged unscathed. He was very spiritual and spent hours before joining any warfare in complex rituals and prayers, "preparing his mind and his spirit for battle."

Roman Nose always wore an elaborate eagle feather war bonnet with a single buffalo horn on the front, a gift that was made for him by a respected medicine man. He believed this splendid headdress had magical powers that protected him in battle and made him a victorious warrior. To maintain this power, there were certain rituals and precautions that he had to follow. On this day, Roman Nose was not eager to go into battle because he'd learned that one of the rules required to maintain the protection of his war bonnet had been violated. The medicine man had told Roman Nose he must never eat any food that had touched metal or else he'd be killed in his next battle. Unknowingly, at a recent feast, he'd eaten some bread that had been removed from an iron pot with a metal fork. He'd had no opportunity to complete the purification ceremonies that required several days and were necessary to restore the war bonnet's protective power. He'd remained apart from the other warriors and had not answered the call to battle. Now the other chiefs insisted he join the attack to inspire the young braves, and they refused to listen to his explanations or fears. Roman Nose had reluctantly applied his war paint and donned his war bonnet, although without its protection, he was certain he was a dead man. He rode out to lead the Dog Soldiers in another bold charge.

Forsyth's weary scouts couched in their pits, rifles ready, as another wave of Indians swept toward them. They spotted the tall, well-built Indian on a spirited black war pony, racing toward them, the red and black feather tails of his war bonnet flying behind him. Roman Nose, a legend among the white people as well as Indians, raced back and forth in front of them, followed by a horde of screaming braves. The scouts aimed carefully, and there was a loud crack of their Spencer carbines when the Indians reached the stream's edge. Twice Roman Nose led the charge directly at the frontiersmen and was unscathed by the barrage of bullets. On the third pass at the west end of the sandbar, he suddenly veered aside but didn't fall and turned back toward the northern ridge. When two chiefs went looking for Roman Nose, they found him lying on the ground, staring up at the blue September afternoon sky. He'd been hit in the back near his spine. He was carried back to the Cheyenne village, where he died as the sun came up the following morning. The loss of their war chief took the heart out of the young braves, and the wails and cries of the Sioux and Cheyenne women rent the air. His death caused the other chiefs to change their battle plan from attack to siege.

As night fell, Forsyth knew they couldn't escape the encircling Indians; they had no horses, rations were running low, and they were vastly outnumbered. Their only hope of survival was to get help, so he asked for volunteers to

Roman Nose Monument above the west end of the sandbar, where the feared leader of the Cheyenne Dog Soldiers was killed by frontiersmen. *Courtesy of Tom Williams.*

Roman Nose always led Cheyenne Dog Soldiers in daring charges back and forth within rifle range of troops. His tall, impressive build was easily recognized. Harper's New Monthly Magazine, *June 1895. Public domain.*

try to slip through the Indians and walk miles back to Fort Wallace. Jack Stillwell and an older fur trapper, Pierre Trudeau, stepped forward. They took Forsyth's only map, a compass, a few provisions, and canteens filled with stagnant river water and slipped away into the darkness. In an attempt to hide the direction they were going, they walked backward in their stocking feet, with their boots tied together and looped around their necks. They stumbled through the night and hid from roaming Indians during the day. Once when there was no place to hide on the bare, open prairie, they crawled inside the dried-up carcasses of two dead buffalos.

On the second day of the siege, arrows continued to whiz into the scouts' pits; bullets kicked up sand or ripped through the rotting horse carcasses. Forsyth thought grimly about their odds of survival: 19 scouts were wounded and 2 were dead. The third day brought more of the same, but their rations were gone, and their pack animals with the supplies had been driven off by the Indians. One scout named Hurst wrote, "Had nothing to eat but the dead horses which were festering and decaying about us, and when you cut into meat, the stench was something frightful and it had green streaks running all through it." They sprinkled gunpowder over the rotten flesh to counter its awful taste, but some men could no longer eat anything and retched at the sight of the putrid horsemeat.

Unsure of the fate of the first two messengers, Forsyth sent out two more volunteers, Scott Donovan and Allison Philey. They wore moccasins to hide their trail and headed south that night toward Cheyenne Wells. Everyone listened as the two slipped away, and when there were no triumphant shouts from the Indians, the trapped men breathed sighs of relief—maybe the messengers would get through. The besieged frontiersmen could only hope and watch the horizon for help that might eventually come. By the fourth day, a small charge of Indians could have overrun the exhausted men and taken the island, but the Cheyenne had lost too many warriors and preferred to starve the scouts. Many abandoned the fight and drifted away as the women dismantled the village and prepared to move on. The scouts stayed in their fortified positions because they could not move the wounded men without horses, and they feared an ambush. The stench of the rotting carcasses was unbearable as blowflies buzzed around the bloated animals and tormented the wounded scouts. These men suffered in their sand pits on the narrow 40-by-200-foot sandbar, where there was no relief from the blazing sun.

On the eighth day, scout Chauncey Whitney wrote in his diary, "Made some soup tonight from putrid horse flesh. My God! Have you deserted us?" On the morning of the ninth day, most of the Indians seemed to have lost interest in finishing off the scouts and moved on. Whitney wrote in his diary, "Arose at daylight to feel all the horrors of starvation slowly but surely approaching. Got a light breakfast of horse meat."

That was the last meal of horsemeat for the scouts because help finally arrived with the Tenth Cavalry Buffalo Soldiers. It was September 25 when one of the scouts shouted, "By the God above us, it's our boys!" as he pointed to a column of troops and a field ambulance on the eastern horizon. The Indians, who were concealed along the stream, fled when the

*Right*: Major George A. "Sandy" Forsyth, Civil War veteran, was wounded three times but survived the nine-day siege of the Battle at Beecher Island in Colorado Territory. *Library of Congress.*

*Below*: The original monument 200 yards south was washed away in the 1935 Arikaree River Flood. Only a portion of the engraved base was recovered. *Courtesy of History Colorado.*

soldiers approached. As Lieutenant Colonel Carpenter and Company H splashed across the shallow Arikaree, the dark faces of the Buffalo Soldiers beamed beneath their floppy campaign hats. Forsyth later wrote, "There was a wild cheer that made the little valley ring as strong men grasped hands and flung their arms around each other and they laughed and cried." When Colonel Carpenter approached Forsyth as he lay helpless in his sand pit, the major was so overcome with emotion that he just looked down at his book, "pretending to read Oliver Twist." He later explained that "it was only an

The death of Roman Nose, a powerful war chief, was a great blow to the Cheyenne, whose young braves eagerly followed him into battle. *Public domain, 1865 Stereoscopic view.*

affectation though for I had all I could do to keep from breaking down…sore and feverish and tired and hungry."

Reuben Waller, a former slave and an original member of the Tenth Cavalry, who'd enlisted with Colonel Carpenter in 1867, rode onto the sandbar with him. Years later, he recalled, "What a sight we saw—30 wounded and dead right in the middle of 50 dead horses that had lain there in the hot sun for ten days. And these men had been eating that putrid flesh of those dead horses for ten days! The men were in dying condition when Carpenter and myself dismounted and began to rescue them."

Some of the Buffalo Soldiers started cooking fires and brewed broth for those who were unable to eat solid rations. As they spooned the nourishing liquid into the mouths of the weakest, Reuben said, "We began to feed the men from our haversacks. If the doctor had not arrived in time, we would have killed them by feeding them to death. The men were eating all we gave them." Waller continued, "We all cried together as we helped them out of their starving condition. God bless the Beecher Island men. They were a noble set of men."

The Black soldiers cared for the wounded scouts, cleaning wounds that were infested with maggots and applying bandages. Tents were set up a distance away from the stench of the dead horses, and the wounded men were moved there. The bodies of the six frontiersmen were buried on the island. The survivors learned that all four messengers had managed to reach

Beecher Island Battlefield Monument, a joint Colorado-Kansas Historical site established in 1905 on a low ridge overlooking the sandbar site on Arikaree. *Courtesy of Tom Williams*.

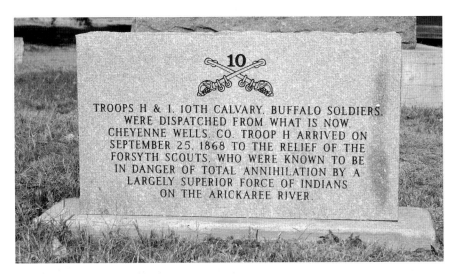

Monument to Lieutenant Fred Beecher, who was killed here with five frontiersmen. The battlefield was once marked by hundreds of horse skeletons. *Courtesy of Tom Williams.*

Fort Wallace or found troops in the field. Two rescue parties had been sent from the fort, but Carpenter and the Buffalo Soldiers were the first to reach the men on the sandbar. They named the place Beecher Island after their young officer, who was one of the first to die. After three days of rest, the most seriously wounded men were loaded into the ambulance, and the troop started back to Fort Wallace. They saw no Indians on their return journey, and the patients received plenty of solicitous care from their Black comrades.

Major Forsyth estimated that 800 to 1,000 Cheyenne and Lakota Sioux had attacked his force of 50 men, killing 6. There were 19 wounded, and all of the horses and mules had been killed or taken by the Indians. Since the Cheyenne usually removed their dead and wounded from the battlefield, Forsyth could only estimate that 9 to 32 Indians had been killed, although many thought the number was much greater. Months after their ordeal, when their wounds had healed, the survivors of Beecher Island took the Buffalo Soldiers out for a wild night of drinking and celebration far from Fort Wallace.

On October 22, 1868, just two weeks after the Beecher Island rescue, Colonel Carpenter and two companies of Buffalo Soldiers escorted Major Eugene Carr into the field to locate the Fifth Cavalry. Carr was to take over command of that regiment, which was out on patrol. Suddenly, a war party of more than 500 Cheyenne came screaming over a hill and shooting into their ranks.

Colonel Carpenter extends a helping hand to Major Forsyth after the Tenth Cavalry Buffalo Soldiers drove off the Cheyenne, ending the nine-day siege at Beecher Island. Harper's New Monthly Magazine, *June 1895, Public domain.*

Fighting off the Indians, Carpenter and the troopers worked their way toward Beaver Creek, where the teamsters pulled the supply wagons into a circle. The Buffalo Soldiers quickly rode inside, jumped off their horses, formed a firing line at the gaps between the wagons, and sent massive volleys at the waves of Indians. These Buffalo Soldiers were skilled marksmen, and the barrage of bullets from their seven-shot repeating rifles decimated the first attackers. The Indians dismounted and used their ponies as barriers, but the guns of the troopers were as effective as cannon fire. Only three braves made it to within 50 yards of the wagons before they were shot down. A second body of Indians closed in, trying to attack from the front, rear, and both flanks, but they were driven back and lost many warriors. Finally, the Indians had enough, and the rest of the war party turned and rode off.

Later Carpenter sent out scouts, who eventually located the Fifth Cavalry, and after delivering Major Carr and the troop's supplies, the joking, triumphant Tenth Cavalrymen rode back to Fort Wallace. Carpenter and the Buffalo Soldiers had been in the field one week, ridden 230 miles, and routed at least 500 Indians, killing many. Three soldiers were wounded. In official dispatches to the War Department, General Sheridan commended Carpenter and the Buffalo Soldiers of the Tenth Cavalry for the "gallantry and bravery displayed by this small company against so large a body of Indians." Carpenter was promoted to a full colonel, and years later, in 1898, he was awarded the Medal of Honor for his actions at Beecher Island and Beaver Creek in 1868. He was one of seven Tenth Cavalry soldiers who would receive this honor for their frontier service. Major Carr, who'd refused to serve with these Black troops in 1866, praised their courage and said, "The Buffalo Soldiers saved my hair!"

# SHERIDAN'S WINTER CAMPAIGN, NOVEMBER 1868–FEBRUARY 1869

General Phil Sheridan, who'd replaced Sherman as commander of the Department of the Missouri, realized that summer campaigns against the Indians were not effective. There was plenty of food available for them then, and the Indians were able to attack swiftly and move on to their next target. When they were waging war in the warmer months, the Cheyenne usually moved their families across the plains with the warriors, but the frigid cold and blizzards made winter travel difficult. The ground was frozen, and the grass was dried up, so their ponies had poor forage during the winter. Game was scarce, the buffalo were gone, and food was in short supply, so the tribes remained in their camps until the spring.

Sheridan developed a four-pronged plan for a winter campaign to drive the Native Americans from their homes and force them onto the reservations in Indian Territory, clearing the plains for settlement. Several large columns of infantry and cavalry would approach from different directions, sweep across the plains, driving the scattered tribes east in front of them. Then the columns would come together in a pincher action to force the hostile Plains tribes to surrender and go to the reservations or face starvation.

In the fall of 1868, some companies of the Tenth Cavalry were scattered around Indian Territory, but others remained in Kansas to guard its western border. Five companies went to Camp Supply in Indian Territory, which would become a supply depot during the winter campaign. The Buffalo Soldiers built neat log structures for barracks and storehouses for supplies, ammunition, and stables. Tons of grain and wagonloads of hay from the fields around Fort Gibson were stored for the cavalry horses at Camp Supply. The troopers knew this campaign would be hard on their horses, so this fort would be used for the rest and reconditioning of animals that survived. In November, four companies of Buffalo Soldiers were transferred to Fort Lyon, on the plains of southeastern Colorado near Bent's Fort. These troops were to keep the Cheyenne on their small, barren reservation nearby and prevent them from moving farther west or north.

General Sheridan launched the Winter Campaign of 1868–69 when he gave the Tenth Cavalry Buffalo Soldiers at Fort Lyon their marching orders. Commanded by Brigadier General W.H. Penrose and with "Wild Bill" Hickok as scout, their column set out on November 10 with 43 days' rations and headed east toward the Canadian River in Texas. Here they would meet a column of Fifth Cavalry troops led by General Carr that was pushing southeast with supply wagons. The Buffalo Soldiers would replenish their supplies here and then continue east. Unfortunately, after only 5 days, the Tenth Cavalry troops were struck by a fierce blizzard. Trails and landmarks were obscured, and it was so cold that soldiers could not hold the reins in their frostbitten hands—their toes and feet lost all sensation. The snow was blinding, and the drifts were so deep that General Penrose was forced to stop and make camp in a barren, open space where there was neither wood nor buffalo chips for warming fires. The wind

Flimsy canvas tents like this Fort Garland model offered little protection against frigid cold and howling blizzards. *Courtesy of Tom Williams.*

howled all night around the soldiers' miserably cold canvas tents, but the next morning, they were ready to resume the struggle. The blizzard piled up snow drifts so deep that their horses couldn't get through, so they dismounted and trudged on, leading their exhausted animals. If a horse collapsed, it was left behind to freeze in the below-zero weather.

By December 6, the Buffalo Soldiers hadn't located General Carr and the supply wagons and were reduced to quarter rations. There was no hay or forage for the horses. Private James Massey recalled, "Twenty-five horses gave out, in weather so cold they froze to death standing on the picket line. Every man who lost his horse had to march with his saddle on his back. We run short of rations, was without anything to eat, except for quarter rations for three or four days." Still the Buffalo Soldiers pushed on, losing even more horses, as many as 14 in one day.

As the temperature remained far below zero, many suffered frostbite of their fingers and toes. Despite their desperate situation, the Black troops remained cheerful, rubbing their hands and feet to warm them. At night, they crafted makeshift footgear from the hides of their horses to replace leather boots that had fallen apart.

Meanwhile, General Carr and his troops, guided by Buffalo Bill Cody, had run into another howling blizzard and weather so cold that three soldiers froze to death. Their herd of 200 cattle, which was the troops' meat supply for the expedition, perished in the deep snow drifts. Carr's rations were running low, too. When they finally found Major Carr, the Buffalo Soldiers were slowly starving on quarter rations, and more than 200 horses had died from starvation. Carr combined the cavalry camps, and after they had sufficient rest and food, he selected 500 soldiers who were in the best condition and continued to push east toward the Canadian River. They reached it on December 28 and remained there until January 8, when they were joined by General Penrose and the remaining troops. They learned that another column of troops had pushed a large force of Comanches east from New Mexico and then defeated them in a battle at the Red River on Christmas Day. As part of the Winter Campaign, General Sheridan had assigned Colonel Custer and the Seventh Cavalry to roam the plains and engage the scattered Indian bands in combat whenever possible. Sheridan issued orders to "destroy villages and ponies, to kill or hang all warriors, and to bring back all woman and children survivors." Custer had wiped out Black Kettle's camp on the Washita River in Indian Territory and killed the peace chief. These military actions had taken place while soldiers with Carr and Penrose were struggling through blizzards.

While they were camped on the Canadian River, General Penrose issued a written statement praising the Buffalo Soldiers and their officers, saying that through their endurance and suffering, they had pushed a large body of Indians into the Seventh Cavalry's path, causing their defeat. He extended his "kindest heartfelt thanks and best wishes for success in all their future endeavors." The Tenth Cavalrymen appreciated this acknowledgment of their important contribution to the success of Sheridan's Winter Campaign.

The Buffalo Soldiers who'd remained behind in Kansas had many more battles with the Cheyenne and Pawnees. Colonel Carpenter and the tough men who'd made the Beecher Island rescue scoured the area south of the Arkansas River for war parties and patrolled around the Republican River, Beecher Island, the Arikaree, and Big Sandy until the Winter Campaign ended in February 1869.

Early one morning in March 1869, Colonel Carpenter's Tenth Cavalry troopers sat easily in their saddles, now seasoned veterans waiting for the bugle call and the order to move out. They were heading for Camp Wichita in Indian Territory, near a site that Sheridan had selected for a new post. He'd put Colonel Carpenter and his men in charge of building the place, which would be named Fort Sill after a Union army general killed in the Civil War.

# 5

# THE BATTLE OF SUMMIT SPRINGS, 1869, AND THE RED RIVER WAR, 1874–75

amp Wichita in Indian Territory became the Tenth Cavalry's regimental headquarters in March 1869, with Colonel Grierson as the first commander. The regiment's troops had been widely scattered in 1868, and eight companies of Buffalo Soldiers had gone to the Texas Panhandle, where they endured miserable conditions in Sheridan's Winter Campaign. Soldiers had suffered frostbite, which led to amputations of toes and feet, and resulted in permanent disability. Many developed scurvy due to their poor diet during months in the field. The exhausted troopers were looking forward to a change, but Colonel Carpenter and his men knew if they wanted a more comfortable post, they would have to build it.

The troops constructed sturdy buildings, using large blocks of stone from local quarries instead of the usual adobe bricks and cottonwood logs. Spaced around the parade ground, they built officers' quarters, enlisted men barracks, stables, and storehouses, but their progress was often interrupted by their expeditions against the Kiowa, Pawnee, Comanche, and Cheyenne, who repeatedly fled the reservation. Colonel Grierson described Sheridan's Winter Campaign as a "grand fizzle" that cost the lives of many soldiers and caused the deaths of hundreds of horses. By the spring of 1869, the Southern Cheyenne were once again roaming the plains, and the fierce Dog Soldiers were firmly entrenched in the prime buffalo country around the Republican River.

Tenth Cavalry troops knew that if they wanted a warm barracks like this, they would have to build it themselves. *Courtesy of Tom Williams.*

# 1869 ARMY REORGANIZATION

In 1867, at the height of the Indian Wars, the army foolishly stopped recruiting men, despite the dire need for additional troops in the West. Congress directed military commanders not to replace soldiers who'd been killed or severely wounded until each company was reduced to only 50 privates. In 1869, Congress ordered the consolidation of the Black infantry regiments, reducing their number from six to four.

To accomplish this consolidation, the Thirty-Eighth Infantry marched from Kansas and New Mexico to Fort McKavett, Texas, where their units were combined with the Forty-First Regiment to become the Twenty-Fourth Infantry, commanded by Colonel Ranald Mackenzie. The Thirty-Ninth and Fortieth Regiments came from the South and were combined into the Twenty-Fifth Infantry, commanded by Colonel Joseph Mower. The Buffalo Soldiers in these two combined infantry regiments remained in Texas, where they manned several posts and served alongside the men of the Ninth Cavalry.

## BATTLE OF SUMMIT SPRINGS

In May 1869, Major Carr and the Fifth Cavalry troops from Fort Lyon surprised a village of Tall Bull's Dog Soldiers on the eastern plains of Colorado. They killed 23 braves and followed the band as it fled north, raiding settlers, stages, and railroad crews in their path. They captured a young woman, Maria Weichell, burned her cabin, and then raided the nearby Alderdice homestead. They took Susanna Alderdice and her three-month-old baby girl prisoner after killing three of her young sons and severely wounding her four-year-old son, Willis.

When Tom Alderdice returned from Salina, Kansas, where he'd gone to file a homestead claim, he found his young son barely alive with five arrows firmly lodged in his back. Willis survived, but Alderdice was devastated by the loss of his other children, the kidnapping of his wife, and the destruction of their home. Following the Cheyenne's trail, he found the body of his baby daughter dangling from a tree limb. The infant was strangled and

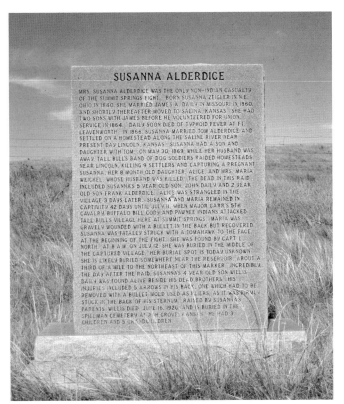

Monument to Susanna Alderdice, held captive 42 days by Tall Bull's Cheyenne Dog Soldiers. She was killed when Fifth Cavalry attacked Indian camp. She was buried in the area by troopers. *Courtesy of Tom Williams.*

Original Monument to the Battle of Summit Springs on July 11, 1869. The Fifth Cavalry with 300 troops and 50 Pawnee scouts, led by Buffalo Bill Cody, attacked the Indian camp. *Courtesy of Tom Williams.*

Battle of Summit Springs memorial: "This monument erected by concerned members of both the red and white races in the Moon of Black Cherries, August 1970." *Courtesy of Tom Williams.*

tossed there for the buzzards. The grief-stricken frontiersman, who'd survived the siege of Beecher Island, spent many months searching for his wife, Susanna.

Colonel Carr and the Fifth Cavalry with 50 Pawnee scouts and guide Buffalo Bill Cody trailed Tall Bull around eastern Colorado for a month. These Dog Soldiers and their families decided to join the Sioux in Nebraska, but they delayed two days before trying to cross the Platte River because the water was very high. They camped near Summit Springs and waited for the river to recede. Meantime, Carr's Pawnee scouts, who were lifelong enemies of the Cheyenne, followed their trail and discovered Tall Bull's large camp.

On July 11, 1869, under cover of a heavy fog, Carr's troops attacked the unsuspecting Cheyenne. The surprised Indians scattered wildly as the braves raced to catch their horses so they could be mounted, ready to fight. The women and children fled to the nearby bluffs, where they tried to hide, but they were chased down and slaughtered by the merciless Pawnees. All of the Cheyenne Dog Soldiers wore long, elaborately decorated scarves

Tall Bull's Lodge site. Alderdice was killed, and captive Maria Weichell was severely wounded by Indians here. The Cheyenne camp was destroyed, 50 Indians were killed, and few prisoners were taken. *Courtesy of Tom Williams.*

around their waists, which trailed on the ground. In time of battle, each warrior would take a stand, impale his scarf to the ground and fight to the death. Tall Bull took his final stand and began the song only members of this warrior society could sing as the screaming Pawnees swarmed over him.

Susanna Alderdice was killed by her captors, and Maria Weichell was severely wounded. Carr's 244 cavalrymen surrounded the Cheyenne, and the fierce fight ended with Tall Bull and 52 Cheyenne dead, 17 women and children taken prisoner, and more than 300 Indian ponies and mules recovered. Only 1 trooper was wounded.

A few Cheyenne managed to escape at Summit Springs: some fled north to the Black Hills, while others went south to surrender at Fort Sill and join the Southern Cheyenne on their reservation. The Battle of Summit Springs ended the Dog Soldiers' influence as a fighting force among the Plains tribes. Despite this Cheyenne defeat, it would be years before the eastern region of the Colorado Territory would be safe for settlers. Indian trouble continued, and in 1871, Colonel Carpenter and two troops of Buffalo Soldiers captured Kiowa war chiefs Satank, Big Tree, and Satanta.

# DESTRUCTION OF THE BUFFALO HERDS

By the winter of 1873, the Plains tribes were in crisis because the United States had once again broken the treaty and failed to deliver the promised supplies or food. The starving tribes were forced to flee the reservations to hunt for meat to survive, but the buffalo herds, once their main food source,

Plains across the West, like these near Summit Springs, Colorado, were once home to huge herds of buffalo, which were vital to the Indians' way of life. *Courtesy of Tom Williams.*

were being rapidly destroyed by professional buffalo hunters. The Tenth Cavalry spent the cold winter of 1873–74 in a futile effort trying to force the Indians back to the reservations.

# RED RIVER WAR, 1874–75

In the winter of 1874–75, General Sheridan launched a campaign to remove the Comanche, Kiowa, Southern Cheyenne, and Arapaho from the Texas Panhandle and relocate them on reservations in Indian Territory. Five columns of troops approached the Red River and its tributaries in the Panhandle from the north, south, east, and west. The Buffalo Soldiers of the Ninth and Tenth Cavalries and the Twenty-Fifth Infantry joined several white cavalry regiments and surrounded the region. They eliminated the Indians' escape routes, destroyed their camps, food, clothing, and drove them onto the reservations. The Buffalo Soldiers and other troopers fought more than 20 battles, and endured miserable conditions without enough food or forage for their horses. As their animals collapsed from hunger and

*Left*: Apache scouts and the Buffalo Soldiers of the Ninth and Tenth Cavalry pursued Victorio for two years, until he was killed in 1880. *Courtesy of Fort Huachuca Museum.*

*Below*: Soldiers suffered terribly from the cold and frostbite on winter marches and dreamed of warm barracks like this one at Fort Garland, Colorado. *Courtesy of Tom Williams.*

exhaustion, the troopers were forced to plod along on foot, carrying their saddles on their backs. Some were so weak they had to be supported by their comrades. They didn't have warm clothing that was adequate for the frigid weather, and their boots were soon in shreds. Dozens of soldiers developed severe frostbite on their feet and toes, which led to amputation. Hundreds of horses froze to death, and both man and beast suffered intensely before the miserable winter campaign ended in February. Commanders who'd never worked with the Black troops before heaped praise on these men. In his report to the War Department, Colonel Buell wrote, "I cannot give the Buffalo Soldiers too much credit for manly endurance without complaint."

The Red River War of 1874–75 was a turbulent turning point in the history of the frontier. The numerous battles and skirmishes waged by more than 3,000 soldiers in the Texas Panhandle forced the outnumbered warriors and their families to spend the winter months fleeing and fighting. The Southern Plains Indians finally gave up their free-roaming way of life and returned to their reservations in June 1875.

The Tenth Cavalry moved to West Texas to battle the fierce Mescalero and Lipan Apaches. Working with the Twenty-Fourth and Twenty-Fifth Infantries, they built 300 miles of roads and laid over 200 miles of telegraph lines in 1875. They scouted 34,420 miles of the desolate West Texas terrain and made maps that were invaluable to the military and settlers.

In 1880, the Buffalo Soldiers went to the Arizona Territory to pursue the Apache leader, Victorio, who fled from the San Carlos reservation. His band of renegades raided throughout eastern Arizona, New Mexico, and Texas, and then escaped into Mexico. When Victorio tried to return to New Mexico, the cavalry drove him back across the border, where he was killed by Mexican troops in October 1880.

By 1885, the Tenth Cavalry was pursuing Geronimo in the Arizona Territory, and after his surrender in 1886, the regimental headquarters were moved to Fort Whipple near Prescott, the territorial capital. A detachment of Tenth Cavalry Buffalo Soldiers fought one of their last battles of the Apache Wars near the Salt River in March 1890. In 1891, after 20 years of service in the Southwest, the Tenth Cavalry was transferred to the Department of Dakota.

# 6

# THE NINTH CAVALRY

## *"We Can, We Will!"*

Recruits for the Ninth Cavalry trained in Louisiana, and in March 1867, they sailed to Texas, where they would remain for the next eight years. Their commander, Colonel Edward Hatch, had served in the Civil War with Colonel Grierson's cavalry raid through Mississippi. When the Ninth's troops reached Texas, they found the forts, which had been built around 1849, were old, deteriorated adobe buildings with leaking, thatched roofs. Time and weather had taken a toll on these posts, which had been abandoned when the Union troops were withdrawn at the beginning of the Civil War.

Colonel Hatch took over the run-down regimental headquarters at Fort Stockton and put crews to work repairing the officers' quarters and building new barracks for the enlisted men. These structures would replace the flimsy lean-to shelters that had no floors, windows, or doors and didn't protect the soldiers from the weather. The troopers learned how to repair disintegrating adobe walls, replace rotten, warped woodwork in the barracks, and construct sturdy roofs that didn't leak. They worked all day under the blazing sun, and when darkness came, they ate their bacon and beans, then crawled into their tents or slept outside on the ground. The work was hard, and the troops' situation couldn't be improved quickly, so they continued to live in inadequate makeshift barracks, tents, barns, and shacks. Most of the recruits endured the bitterly cold winter nights rolled up in blankets as they tried to sleep in drafty canvas tents. A year after the cavalry's arrival at Fort Davis, Texas, only two new barracks had been built, but the soldiers who were

The Ninth Cavalry had to rebuild most abandoned forts in Texas before they had decent living quarters. Building was often interrupted by battles with Indians. *Courtesy of Tom Williams.*

lucky enough to get a place inside were thankful to be under a roof, even if it did leak! They ignored the dirt floor that turned into a muddy mire when it rained and were glad to be snug and warm on iron bedsteads, while the others still slept in tents.

An inspecting officer at Fort Quitman found companies of the Ninth Cavalry and the Twenty-Fourth and Twenty-Fifth Infantries living in adobe barracks with low ceilings, dirt floors, and leaky roofs. He reported, "In rainy weather, the quarters leak a good deal and are not only uncomfortable but very unhealthful—as the water does not cease dripping from the ceiling for some time after the storm or shower has passed away." The appalled inspector concluded, "It is a great evil to keep troops too long at any of these posts where the accommodations are so bad." Little did he know that the Ninth Cavalry Buffalo Soldiers would be stationed in these Texas forts for eight years, and the Twenty-Fourth Infantry would remain even longer.

As late as 1873, when a company of the Ninth Cavalry and Twenty-Fourth Infantry arrived at Fort McIntosh, Texas, the repairs on the barracks still hadn't been completed. The cavalry moved into a storehouse and the infantry was quartered in the hospital; the ill patients were sent to "a hired house in the dirty little town of Laredo a mile distant." Three years later, the cavalry was gone; the infantry had moved into the storehouse, and the hospital was once again available for patients, saving the government the expense of renting a house in town.

West Texas was overrun by Mescalero and Lipan Apaches, Comanches, Kiowas, and Kickapoos, whose frequent attacks on migrants, stages, and wagon trains had prevented permanent settlement of the region. The Twenty-Fourth and Twenty-Fifth Infantries bolstered the strength of the Ninth Cavalry, but there still weren't enough troops to patrol such a vast territory. These inexperienced soldiers weren't prepared for the lightning-fast Indian raids, and at first, they had little success fighting off the war parties. However, once they became accustomed to the harsh Texas environment and familiar with the Indians' warfare tactics, they had more success. The Native Americans often evaded capture or defeat by fleeing over the Mexican border, and because there was no agreement between the two governments, the cavalry could not pursue them.

## ATTACK ON FORT LANCASTER, DECEMBER 26, 1867

Fort Lancaster, a rundown fort that squatted along the San Antonio–El Paso Road, was being slowly rebuilt by the 58 men of K Company, commanded by Captain William Frohock. The post's protective outer wall had crumbled away, its gates had fallen down, and all the dilapidated buildings were collapsing. Late in the afternoon of December 26, 1867, a mounted guard detail moved the company's horses and mules from their grazing area to water at a creek near the fort. Three civilians and a teamster were busy filling water barrels for the post and didn't see the two large groups of Kickapoos stealthily approaching. The Indians attacked quickly, killing the teamster and two troopers, but the rest of the herders managed to drive the horses into the fort. Because the outer walls were just piles of rubble, the Kickapoos raced right through the center of the compound, shooting and yelling. The horses milled around, adding to the chaos, as the outnumbered troopers maintained steady gunfire with their .50-caliber Spencer rifles. Suddenly, the herd of horses bolted out of the fort, and the Indians stopped shooing to chase the coveted animals.

Angry about losing the horses, Captain Frohock and a large group of Buffalo Soldiers followed the Kickapoos on foot, and they were soon engaged in another fight. The Indians stayed out of the 200-yard range of the soldiers' Spencer carbines, swiftly rounded up the horses, and raced off.

The sound of gunfire sent the troopers running back to see a huge war party of about 900 Kickapoos ready to overrun the small group of soldiers guarding the post. As arrows whizzed through the air, and bullets ripped into the fort's old adobe walls, Captain Frohock's wife and her sister filled their aprons with cartridges and passed the ammunition to the defenders, who were firing from the doorways and windows of the outbuildings. Several more large groups of Kickapoos watched from the surrounding hills but

Fort Lancaster was a pile of rubble when Kickapoos attacked in 1867. It took years to build a secure post of adobe bricks. *Courtesy of Tom Williams.*

didn't join the fight. As the day wore on, the Indians began to drift away after losing 20 braves. Three Buffalo Soldiers were killed, and 32 cavalry horses and 6 mules were stolen.

The next morning, while his inexperienced troops roamed around collecting arrows, a war bonnet, and assorted battle souvenirs, Frohock sent a message to regimental headquarters at Fort Stockton: "I have the honor to report that my camp was attacked from three directions by upwards of nine hundred Indians, Mexicans and white renegades about 4 '0' clock P.M. yesterday. The new enlisted men, especially the noncommissioned officers, behaved gallantly." He continued, "The men of the 9th Cavalry and the two infantry regiments are quickly becoming seasoned fighters in Texas."

# EXPLORATIONS OF GUADALUPE MOUNTAINS

The fierce Mescalero Apaches repeatedly attacked settlers and soldiers and then quickly retreated to their remote hideouts in the rugged, unexplored Guadalupe Mountains of southwestern Texas. The Ninth Cavalry's commander, Colonel Hatch, was determined to penetrate this Indian stronghold, and he reasoned that once troops had invaded their fortress, the Apaches wouldn't feel as secure and might decrease their attacks on white people.

In January 1870, Captain Francis Dodge and 200 men of the Ninth Cavalry headed northwest from Fort Davis into the Guadalupe Mountains. A fierce spring storm hit, and as the troopers were slogging through the mud, they stumbled on an Apache camp. The Indians fled, scrambling up the rocky slopes of a nearby peak as the troopers dismounted and pursued them. They inched up the steep incline in the downpour, climbing over slippery boulders under the Apaches' withering gunfire from above. When the troopers reached the summit, they discovered that the Indians had slipped away and disappeared into the maze of canyons below. Disgusted and too exhausted to make their way safely down the mountain in the darkness, the Buffalo Soldiers huddled together and endured a frigid night on the rocky peak. The next morning, they limped down the mountain, retrieved their horses, and resumed the search. They found only an abandoned Apache camp, which they destroyed along with its stockpile of food and supplies, and then they headed back to Fort Davis.

On April 13, 1870, Major Morrow and 91 men of the Ninth Cavalry set out from Fort Quitman to scout in the Guadalupe Mountains, where they were soon lost in the confusing spiderweb of Apache trails. They wandered about until they found themselves trapped in a deep, impassable box canyon and spent hours searching for a way out. Every side canyon dead-ended in a solid rock wall. Finally, a scout discovered a hidden passage that was almost completely blocked by towering boulders, which they would have to climb to get out of the box canyon. The horses could not do this, so the resourceful cavalrymen made slings to lift the animals up and over the boulders and then lower them down the other side. The terrified animals struggled and kicked as they were strapped into the slings, and some almost tumbled out, but the troopers persisted, and as they hauled the last horse up and over, they let out a loud cheer. They lost only one animal because it thrashed so violently that it fell from the sling into a deep crevice. No matter how hard they tried, they weren't able to pull that horse out. Thankful to escape the box canyon, the troopers moved deeper into the mountains and found another abandoned Apache camp, which they burned.

A week later, Captain Dodge and his men were once again lost in a remote region of the Guadalupes. Their exhausted horses had no forage and had been existing on sparse clumps of weeds until they collapsed, unable to continue on. More than half of the cavalrymen had lost their mounts and were on foot. The others were leading their weakened horses, hoping they wouldn't give out. After tramping through miles of cactus and rocks, the soldiers' leather boots were falling apart, and their clothing was in tatters, providing no protection from the cold nights. They found a sheltered arroyo, where they rested for two days and tried to regain their strength, eating their meager supply of hardtack, bacon, and coffee. They mended their ragged clothes and made horsehide moccasins for their bruised, bloody feet before they moved out slowly, limping east, where they hoped to find the Penasco River in this unmapped region.

After working their way out of the Guadelupes, the soldiers found themselves in a barren desert bordering the mountains. They trudged through the dry desert sand in the blast-furnace heat of a sudden early summer, rationing their water, and fighting throat-scorching thirst as shimmering mirages of lakes danced before their eyes. Their canteens were completely dry when they found the shallow Penasco River, which was little more than a stream in a sandy bed. Drinking their fill, they rested one day before resuming their march east, working their way around the Sierra Diablo Mountains, avoiding their rugged, steep slopes and deep canyons. Farther east near Rattlesnake Springs, they surprised a small band of Mescaleros, who fled, leaving 30 lodges and 22 ponies behind, which made the Buffalo Soldiers whoop with relief. Now the boys who'd barely been able to hobble over the rough terrain could ride a half-tame Indian pony. They continued on, and after 53 days, the Buffalo Soldiers finally returned to Fort Quitman. They'd killed only a few Indians, but they'd destroyed their lodges, food, and supplies, which were vital to their survival. More importantly, they'd invaded the Apache stronghold and would map this region, which was no longer an impenetrable hideout.

After these army expeditions into the mountains, the Apache raids on settlers around the Guadalupe Mountains decreased. In his report to the War Department, Major Morrow praised the Ninth Cavalry: "They marched about 1,000 miles, over 200 of which was through country that had never been explored before, they drove the Indians from every rancheria (camp)… destroyed immense amounts of food, robes, skins, utensils, and material, and captured 40 horses and mules. I cannot speak too highly of the conduct of the officers and the men under my command, always cheerful and steady, braving the severest hardships with short rations and no water without a murmur. The negro troops are peculiarly adapted to hunting Indians, knowing no fear and are capable of great endurance."

On May 19, 1870, young Sergeant Emmanuel Stance left Fort McKavett, Texas, with ten cavalrymen to find the Indians who'd stolen horses from their herd. Nearing Kickapoo Springs, the troopers spotted a group of Apaches driving horses through the brush and quickly rushed at them. The surprised braves abandoned the horses and fled. Stance and his men rounded up the animals and rode on to Kickapoo Springs, where they camped for the night. The next morning, on the way back to the fort, they surprised a war party ready to attack a small wagon train. Once again, Stance and his troopers charged, driving off the Indians, rescuing two young boys who had been held captive, and catching five horses. As they were riding back to the fort, the troopers were suddenly attacked from the rear by the war party they'd driven off earlier. Later, Stance reported, "I turned my little command loose on them…and after a few volleys they left me to continue my march in peace." There were no casualties, and the troops reached the fort with all of the recovered horses.

The following day, Stance and his men drove off more Indians and recovered 25 cavalry horses. Captain Carroll, Stance's commanding officer, praised the five-foot-tall sergeant and recommended him for the Congressional Medal of Honor. Emmanuel Stance was the first Buffalo Soldier to be awarded this country's highest military honor for bravery.

In June 1871, Lieutenant Shafter, commander of Fort Davis, set out with 75 Buffalo Soldiers of the Twenty-Fourth Infantry and the Ninth Cavalry to recover 43 horses that had been stolen by Apaches. They followed the Indians' trail into the unexplored, arid White Sands region, which sprawled across the Texas border into New Mexico Territory. The soldiers weren't able to sort out the confusing maze of Indian tracks in the shifting sands, and after two days, they became disoriented as they wandered about in the sand dunes and were soon hopelessly lost. They weren't able to backtrack because the wind quickly blew away any signs of their passing, and there were no landmarks. The blistering sun glared on the sparkling gypsum crystals, blinding them. Their horses were exhausted in the searing heat, and there was no vegetation to provide shade for a much-needed rest. Several troopers developed severe sunburn, increasing their misery. They rationed their water, but after two days, their canteens were empty, and their mouths were as dry as dust. When they stumbled onto a tiny stream running through the dunes, they fell on their knees in thanks, drank their fill, watered their horses, and rested several hours. Then they filled their canteens and trudged on.

For 12 miserable days, the troopers wandered back and forth through the sand dunes, trying to find a way out of this deadly wilderness. The cruel sun poured down, and the relentless heat took its toll as they rationed their water, allowing only a few drops to trickle down their parched throats. Dizzy, swaying riders were tied in their saddles or staggered along on foot, supported by their comrades. When a man fell, he was picked up and carried along by the others. When the sun finally sank below the dunes, the men shuffled about making camp. They tried to eat, but were unable to swallow the dry hard tack or beans and simply collapsed in the sand, dreaming of a cool drink.

Too soon, the dreaded dawn came, and the hot morning sun roused them to face another miserable day. The half-crazed men staggered on, visions of water and icy beverages dancing before their eyes. They dreamed of soothing their swollen tongues and wetting their dry, cracked lips as the hot desert wind seared their skin. Horses tottered, stumbled, fell to the ground and died, leaving more men on foot. As the troopers limped on, the weakest desperately clutched the stirrup strap of a comrade or leaned on the exhausted, lurching horse. After 12 devastating days in White Sands, the dehydrated, exhausted Buffalo Soldiers finally found a way out of the dunes, many miles south of their home fort. They headed north through the barren West Texas plains, and weeks later, they finally stumbled into Fort Davis, much worse for their experience. Lieutenant Shafter reported to the Army Department that the Buffalo Soldiers had shown that they could operate in harsh, barren country and could survive in dangerous territory like White Sands. He said, "Never again could an Indian or Comanchero close his eyes with any guarantee of unbroken sleep in forbidding White Sands."

The Buffalo Soldiers began mapping their expeditions in 1869, when Colonel Hazen led the first troop of 200 men of the Thirty-Eighth Infantry into the rugged mountains and barren deserts of southwestern New Mexico Territory. In just 60 days, they mapped 1,200 miles of previously unexplored country. In 1871, Colonel Shafter led 70 men of the Ninth Cavalry and the Twenty-Fifth Infantry who mapped 500 miles of the territory around Fort Davis. They went as far south as the Rio Grande and the Big Bend Country near the Mexican border. Four years later, in 1875, Shafter and 400 Black troopers of the Twenty-Fourth Infantry mapped 2,500 miles in Texas in just four months. These maps provided crucial information that helped the military move troops through the region to fight Indians, track outlaws, and eventually bring the area under control. The West Texas frontier was finally opened to permanent settlement and was no longer a safe refuge for Indians.

The Indians increased their attacks on settlers in West Texas during Reconstruction, and by 1865, outlaws and Mexican revolutionaries were roaming the border and the Rio Grande region with no interference from the local law. General Christopher Augur, commander of the Department of Texas, shifted five companies of the Ninth Cavalry to guard crossings of the Rio Grande to stop Indians and outlaws from crossing to safety in Mexico. The criminal element was well-established in West Texas, and the state was overrun by former Confederates who'd taken up careers as outlaws. They spent their time drinking, gambling, robbing, and killing local citizens. These men were in constant conflict with Mexican thieves, who also plundered and robbed in the Texas river country. The white outlaws often bragged about the number of men they'd killed, "not counting Mexicans," while Mexicans claimed they deserved medals for shooting white crooks.

By 1872, the criminal activities of the outlaws and the bloody Indian attacks had citizens in despair. They had lost thousands of horses and cattle, their ranches had been robbed, their homesteads had been burned, and hundreds of settlers had been killed. Merchants, banks, post offices, and businesses were robbed regularly; murders were an everyday event in the small towns. The Texas Rangers had been decommissioned in 1873, during the Reconstruction period, because they'd fought for the Confederacy, and the few remaining local lawmen were overwhelmed, unable to stop the criminals. Some sheriffs and town marshals had even joined forces with the thugs and thieves and ignored their activities. If a crook or murderer was

Black troops experienced a great deal of racial prejudice and violence in Texas, and several were killed by white citizens, who were never punished. *Courtesy of National Archives.*

arrested, the local prosecutor was usually too timid to charge him with a crime. If an outlaw eventually did go to trial, the jurors were often so intimidated by threats from local toughs that they were unwilling to convict the accused.

For two years, Colonel Hatch and the Ninth Cavalry tried to establish some semblance of order in West Texas, but the problems were overwhelming. An agreement between the United States and Mexico still hadn't been reached to allow troops to pursue Indians and outlaws across the Rio Grande, and the border country remained in chaos, controlled by criminals. A jungle of thick brush, 30 miles deep, lined both sides of the Rio Grande and was ideal for the camps of outlaws and Indians. Spies were everywhere, busily reporting troop movements to thieves. The robbing, stealing, and killing by small parties of outlaws continued; the Indians roamed the area freely. Patrols of Black cavalrymen went from ranch to ranch looking for outlaws; other troops were stationed in the small border towns as crime deterrents.

In 1872, General Augur praised the Buffalo Soldiers to the Secretary of War, saying, "The labor and privations of troops in this Department are severe. The cavalry is constantly at work, and it is the kind of work that disheartens as there is little to show for it. Yet their zeal is untiring, and if they do not always achieve success, they always deserve it. I have never seen troops more constantly employed."

## PREJUDICE IN TEXAS

Southerners in West Texas hated Black troops, and their feelings were evident. The Austin *Bellville Countryman* newspaper wrote, "The idea of a gallant and high-minded people being ordered and pushed around by an inferior, ignorant race is shocking to the senses." When a battalion of Black troops passed through San Antonio, the *San Antonio Herald* jeered that they "were as common looking niggers as we have seen." Then the paper gloomily predicted that "frontiersmen would not receive much protection from their sort." West Texas newspaper editors allowed the publication of outrageous lies about the performance of the Black troops in battles, and they were often compared to Texas outlaws. As desperately as the settlers needed protection from the Indians and outlaws, they did not welcome help from the Buffalo Soldiers. After a successful action by the Ninth Cavalry against the Comanches, the May 23, 1871 issue of the *San Antonio Herald* taunted, "The Indians are terribly disgusted with the negro troops on the frontier because they are so difficult to scalp."

When Black infantrymen served as stagecoach guards, they were often refused return transportation to the station or their posts and found themselves walking many miles back, alone and easy prey. This dangerous practice continued until the department commander announced that troopers would no longer guard any stages unless they were guaranteed transportation back to their posts. Despite the misery and loss caused by outlaws, local juries rarely convicted a white citizen if he'd been caught by Black troops. If a white person was accused of killing a Black man, odds are that he would not be convicted. There were many instances in which Black soldiers were killed by white men who were never arrested or prosecuted for their crimes. Small detachments of troopers were especially vulnerable to attack by outlaws and white citizens.

In January 1875, five Ninth Cavalry soldiers were camped about 16 miles from Fort Concho when a group of drunk cowboys started racing back and forth nearby, yelling and shooting their guns. The troopers tried to prepare their supper as bullets whistled around their heads. Their Black leader, Sergeant Troutman, believing the shots had come from a nearby ranch house, rode over alone and questioned several heavily armed men who were lounging about. After learning nothing, Troutman and the others decided the wisest course of action was to move on to avoid further trouble. They packed up but had only ridden a short distance when they were shot at again, and a short, vicious gunfight followed in which two privates were killed. Troutman and two other troopers managed to fight their way out of the ambush and make it back to the fort, certain they'd killed at least one of the attackers and wounded a couple others.

The next morning, furious Colonel Hatch rode out to the scene of the gunfight accompanied by a deputy sheriff and 60 troopers. They found the 2 dead soldiers whose bodies had been stripped and horribly mutilated as if they'd been killed by Indians. They discovered the troopers' bloody uniforms and equipment hidden in a nearby shack. Hatch "arrested every suspicious character I could find at the ranch." Two of these men had fresh gunshot wounds, but Hatch gloomily predicted, "Not a jury in the state will convict them." The February 17, 1875 *San Antonio Herald* branded Colonel Hatch a "political trickster...reeking from the stench of radicalism." It added that he was "an incendiary capable of inciting his negro soldiery to do what they are now doing: murder and robbery."

The grand jury at Rio Grande City, Texas, indicted nine of the men for the troopers' murders, but only one man was tried, and he was promptly acquitted. The remaining eight cowboys were released. The three surviving troopers, who were witnesses in the trial, were arrested, thrown in jail and charged with murder for defending themselves when they were ambushed. Colonel Hatch and Lieutenant J. French were indicted for burglary because they had broken into the shack and recovered the bloodstained uniforms of the dead soldiers. Their attorney was granted a change of venue, citing "very great malice in the area" toward Hatch and his men, adding that "their indictments stemmed from gratification of purely local prejudice." Legal fees were expensive for Hatch and the soldiers, but the cost was justified when they were found not guilty and freed. This was just one incident of many illustrating the twisted Texas legal system and the injustice suffered by many Black soldiers.

Frustrated with the persistent lawlessness in West Texas, General Sherman ordered that the Black troops remain at the large main forts instead of being scattered around in small outposts. Governor Coke of Texas pleaded with President Grant to once again allow troops to cross the Rio Grande into Mexico in pursuit of outlaws and Indians, but Grant would not agree, so the raids and crime continued in the border country.

In 1875, Colonel Hatch was ordered to transfer the Ninth Cavalry from Texas to New Mexico Territory. General Sheridan commented that it was time to give the men and officers of the Ninth some relief. The Buffalo Soldiers, whose regimental motto was "We Can, We Will," had served eight years in the worst posts in the West under the most difficult conditions and still handled their duties with courage and determination.

The Black troops were welcomed by the people of New Mexico, who were especially delighted when the Regimental Band arrived at Fort Union. Santa Fe's Music Committee invited the band to participate in the Fourth of July festivities, and when the trip was approved, the city even appropriated $100 for the band's expenses. The bandsmen traveled to the New Mexican capital in two ten-man wagons, taking only their instruments, caps, uniforms, and rations for five days.

The Ninth Cavalry Band was an impressive sight as it stepped out to lead the Fourth of July parade with a rousing march. The crowd cheered loudly when it marched by, its members splendid in their blue uniforms, buttons sparkling, boots polished to a high shine, and their black campaign hats cocked at a jaunty angle.

Sunday afternoon band concerts in Santa Fe's historic Plaza brought families for miles around to sit on the grass and enjoy the music. Their repertoire always included "I'll Take You Home Again, Kathleen," a popular romantic ballad of the time, plus much-loved hymns, patriotic marches, and sprightly tunes. The band's visit to Santa Fe from June 28 to July 13, 1877, was such a great success that the citizens put together a committee of the governor and prominent members of the community to request that it be assigned to Santa Fe's Fort Marcy.

Despite impressive arguments that Marcy was regimental headquarters of the Ninth Cavalry and the Military District in New Mexico, the request was denied. To appease the disappointed citizens, Colonel Hatch sent the band on a performance tour of the remote posts and settlements scattered around the territory. Families and soldiers looked forward to the band's visit, and like the commander at isolated Fort Bayard in southwestern New Mexico, recalled an evening of music with enthusiastic praise for the bandsmen: "They are well up on plantation melodies, as well as the jig and other dances." The *Army Navy Journal* wrote, "A fine minstrel troupe organized by the Ninth Cavalry performed at the post's dance to the applause of a delighted audience of officers, soldiers, and civilians."

In 1880, the Ninth Regimental Band played at a reception in Santa Fe for General Phil Sheridan and remained in the city to perform at several civic events. Once again, crowds gathered in the shade of the Plaza's cottonwood trees on Sunday afternoons to enjoy the concerts. In October 1880, President Rutherford Hayes visited Santa Fe on a transcontinental tour, and when he stepped off the train, the Regimental Band struck up "Hail to the Chief." Then it played lively marches as it led the parade from the depot to the Plaza. Soldiers and citizens cheered patriotic speeches from the president, the governor, Colonel Hatch, the mayor and civic dignitaries. That evening, there was a grand ball for President Hayes, and everyone whirled around the dance floor to the lively reels and romantic waltzes played by these musicians. This evening, undoubtedly, was a once-in-a-lifetime experience for the members of the Ninth Regimental Band, many of whom could recall their days as slaves.

# 7

# THE UTES, TREATIES, AND PROSPECTORS

About 10,000 years ago, the Ute Indians migrated to the Rocky Mountain region and settled in the major river valleys of western Colorado. Hunters and gatherers, the Utes lived a nomadic life and roved north into Wyoming to hunt and traveled south along the Front Range to trade with the Navajos and Jicarilla Apaches in New Mexico. The Arapaho, Cheyenne, and Sioux, who roamed the eastern plains, were their enemies, as were the Kiowas and Comanches in the south.

During the winter, the Utes sought shelter from the cold, snow, and fierce winter blizzards in the warmer valleys along the Western Slope of the Rockies. When the cold loosened its grip, they planted squash, beans, and corn in the rich soil along the rivers and spent the late summer harvesting crops and gathering nuts, fruits, and seeds. In the fall, they spent weeks hunting in the mountains, where there were large herds of deer, elk, and moose. Families accompanied the men who hunted; the women prepared and dried the meat, and tanned the animal hides for tipis, clothing, and moccasins.

The Utes were organized into a loose confederation of bands, and each lived in a general region with traditional winter and summer locations, and a defined hunting territory. Each distinct band had its own chief, who settled all disputes, and whose authority was rarely questioned. The groups were tied together by language, religion, and customs, and they gathered periodically throughout the year. The Uncompahgre Utes lived in the valleys around the Gunnison and Uncompahgre Rivers, and their prime hunting grounds were in the San Juan Mountains. The White River band lived in the river valleys of northwestern Colorado. Three separate bands made up the Southern Utes, who lived in southern Colorado in the foothills of the San Juan Mountains, near the headwaters of the Rio Grande and San Juan Rivers. They roamed as far south as Taos in northern New Mexico and west into southern Utah. The Uintah band lived south of the Great Salt Lake and had little contact with the Utes in Colorado.

Until 1821, Colorado was part of Spain's extensive territory in the Southwest, but early explorers avoided the Western Slope because the Utes were unfriendly. There was little exploration of the region until Don Juan Rivera led a two-year expedition through southern Colorado in 1765–66, looking for silver. These early Spanish prospectors left behind signs of their digging scattered around the San Juan Mountains, and more than a century later, miners found their crude, broken picks and shovels.

In 1776, the year of the Revolutionary War, another Spanish expedition of two Franciscan fathers, Silvestre Escalante and Atanasio Domínguez, led by Juan de Anza, set out from Santa Fe to forge a trail to the California colonies. They traveled through southern Colorado, crossed the Colorado River, and reached the Salt Lake before they were forced to turn back by winter storms.

These early Spaniards brought horses, which the Utes acquired by trading or stealing. They became excellent horsemen, and the animals enhanced their nomadic lifestyle. The rugged mountain men followed the trail made by Zebulon Pike in 1804, when he explored the land acquired in the Louisiana Purchase. In 1821, Mexico won its freedom from Spain and was eager to trade with merchants from the United States. Soon hundreds of wagons loaded with goods were crowding the Santa Fe Trail, the "new commercial highway" to the New Mexican market.

In 1848, Mexico gave up California and a vast amount of land in the Southwest to the United States in the Treaty of Guadalupe Hidalgo. This rapidly changed conditions for the Utes because the U.S. government began encouraging settlement in Colorado on land that had belonged to the Indians for hundreds of years. The angry Utes began raiding tiny settlements and attacking travelers who ventured into the San Luis Valley of southern Colorado. In 1849, alarmed by this hostility, the government called a meeting with Southern Ute leaders and developed a "friendship treaty." Boundaries for Ute lands were drawn up, and the chiefs were told to "cease their rambling habits" and to stay within those borders. The Utes ignored this foolishness from the arrogant white trespassers and continued to roam land that had been theirs for centuries. They resumed their attacks on white and Hispanic settlers.

Flagpole at Fort Garland opened in 1858 to protect San Luis Valley from Indian raids before treaties were developed. *Courtesy of History Colorado.*

In 1852, Fort Massachusetts, the first fort in Colorado, was built to protect settlers in the San Luis Valley, but it was abandoned when Fort Garland was completed in 1858.

The 1859 Pike's Peak gold rush brought thousands of hopefuls to Colorado, but when they didn't strike it rich quickly, most left in disgust. Charles Baker persisted, and in the fall of 1860, his party of prospectors reached the rugged San Juan Mountains in southwestern Colorado. They found flakes and gold dust but were soon forced to leave the mountains by approaching winter storms and frigid cold. They returned the following summer and found small amounts of gold but couldn't locate the source. When the Civil War began, they headed east to join the Confederacy or the Union.

Despite the Civil War, Congress continued to encourage westward migration by passing the Homestead Act of 1862, giving 160 acres of land to anyone who'd make improvements and live on it for five years. The Utes' fertile lands in western Colorado looked especially inviting, but first the pesky Indians had to be pushed onto reservations. If they made trouble, the only alternative would be extermination.

Hoping to impress the Utes with the power of the United States, Territorial Governor Evans sent Ouray, a respected Uncompahgre leader, and 14 chiefs by train on a tour of

Fort Garland was named after General John Garland, commander of Military District of New Mexico. It replaced Fort Massachusetts and operated until 1883. *Courtesy of History Colorado.*

Washington, D.C., and New York City in 1863. They met President Lincoln and went to the circus before returning to the West. Ouray was convinced that the Utes could never defeat the enormous numbers of white people and tried to convince the others that they must compromise with them to survive.

In October 1863, the Utes agreed to give up all of their land east of the Continental Divide in exchange for $20,000 in goods and provisions for the next ten years. Only Ouray, Colorow, and ten Uncompahgre chiefs marked the agreement with their *X*. The other Ute bands refused to honor the agreement because they hadn't been involved in the negotiations. The white settlers weren't satisfied and insisted that all Indians were savages, and their land should just be taken. Trouble continued, and Congress delayed the appropriation of funds for goods promised to the Utes. When the food and herds of cattle and sheep were never delivered in 1864, the starving Utes were reduced to begging for food in the streets of Colorado Springs.

The Utes left their lands to steal cattle and sheep from ranchers, until Congress appropriated the promised funds. Meanwhile, flour and perishable supplies sat in warehouses near the railroad for months instead of being distributed to the Indians, and corrupt officials stole the goods and sold them for a profit. Many conflicts between the Utes and the settlers were directly related to the government's failure to keep its treaty promises. During the severe winter of 1867–68, the promise of rations went unfulfilled in

Fort Garland has been restored and looks as it did in 1858, ten years after the Treaty of Guadalupe Hidalgo greatly increased the nation's size. *Courtesy of Tom Williams.*

Colorado, and angry, hungry Utes roamed about, demanding food from homesteaders and townspeople.

In the spring of 1868, several Ute leaders traveled to Denver to demand that the governor deliver the rations and herds. A month passed, and the Utes were still waiting in the capital, while Denver's citizens made an uproar about 500 Indians roaming the streets. In February 1868, the Ute leaders accompanied Kit Carson on a dazzling tour of several eastern cities, plus Niagara Falls and Washington, D.C., and then hammered out a new agreement, the Kit Carson Treaty. They gave up even more of their traditional lands that were coveted by white settlers. Their new reservation covered the western third of Colorado, and the Indians were assured they "would keep this western Colorado land forever, as long as grass grows and water runs." Again, they were promised annuities of cattle and sheep and $10,000 in cash and $10,000 in food annually for the next 30 years. An agency was established at Los Pinos to serve the Southern and Uncompahgre Utes, while the White River Agency would deal with the White River, Yampa, and Uintah bands in the northwestern part of the territory. All of the Utes present made their mark on this Kit Carson Treaty of 1868.

Buffalo Soldiers standing in the sally port of Fort Garland 1875. They patrolled western Colorado to keep peace between Utes and settlers. *Courtesy of History Colorado.*

Despite this new treaty, again, the promised rations weren't delivered, and the disgusted Utes left the reservation and headed to their favorite hunting regions. Unfortunately, much of this land now belonged to white settlers. When the Utes' rations were delayed, they appeared at far-flung homesteads looking for food. Colorow, a popular chief, had a well-known fondness for biscuits, and many wives grew accustomed to his sudden appearance at their kitchen door, asking for his favorite treat. Some served him biscuits sprinkled

Fort Garland, where Kit Carson was the commanding officer in 1866–67, before retiring for health reasons. He died a year later at Fort Lyon. *Courtesy of Tom Williams.*

with sugar or a spoonful of jam, and Colorow's weight eventually ballooned to over 300 pounds.

In the spring of 1871, prospectors discovered some rocky peaks and exposed cliffs in the San Juan Mountains that were crisscrossed by wide bands of silver. Then they found deposits of gold, which brought hordes trespassing on the Ute hunting grounds. They built their rickety shacks and marred the mountain slopes with their glory holes and piles of tailings. When the protests of the angry Utes were ignored, lone prospectors began to disappear or were attacked. Trouble loomed on the horizon.

Despite the promises made in the 1868 treaty, prospectors had no intention of staying out of the incredibly rich "silvery San Juans." The government offered to buy the entire San Juan district for $25,000 and additional annuities, but the disgusted Utes refused. Tensions increased between the Indians and the trespassers; the Colorado Territorial Legislature made the situation worse by begging the federal government to "just seize the San Juan Mountains!"

In 1872, President Grant ordered a small detachment of Eighth Cavalry troops from Fort Garland to remove all miners from the mountains. The cavalrymen did not have an easy ride into the San Juans, and they struggled to get their heavy supply wagons over precipitous Stony Pass. The climb was steep and rough, and there was little forage for their weary horses and mules. They were met by an angry crowd of armed miners who defied the troops' order to abandon their claims and leave. Knowing they would have a fight on their hands, the Eighth Cavalry quietly turned around and trudged back over the pass. Later that summer, when troops again tried to force the prospectors out of the mountains, only a few left, and they soon returned to resume work on their claims. Pressure was put on the government to develop a new treaty that allowed prospecting in the San Juan Mountains.

Once again, the government's solution was to buy the San Juan Mountains and the southern portion of the Ute reservation, but the Utes refused. Throughout 1873, negotiations continued, and Ouray and a delegation of Utes even spent 60 days in Washington, D.C., trying unsuccessfully to reach an agreement.

# BRUNOT AGREEMENT, SEPTEMBER 1873

Ouray recognized the futility of going to war with the United States and tried to persuade the other leaders that they must compromise again. President Grant appointed a special commission to meet with Ouray, the chiefs of seven Ute bands, and Felix Brunot, chairman of the Board of Indian Commissioners, to discuss the sale of the mining region. On September 13, 1873, after seven days of discussions, the commission announced an arrangement, the Brunot Agreement. The Utes finally agreed to give up about 4 million acres in the mineral-rich San Juan Mountains, which was about one-quarter of their reservation. This left them a 12-million-acre reservation in western Colorado, plus a strip of land along the New Mexico border that became the Southern Ute Reservation. The Indians retained their hunting rights in the San Juan Mountains and the large valleys of Middle and North Parks in the central part of the territory.

From the beginning, there was a misunderstanding, and the Utes believed they were giving up only the mining regions, not the entire San Juan Mountain range. They thought there would not be any permanent buildings in the mountains or on the land around them, but as soon as the Brunot Agreement was signed, the San Juan Mountains experienced a great mining rush. A flood of settlers, merchants, and businessmen quickly established towns that became supply centers for the booming mining camps.

Next, homesteaders demanded that the Utes leave the Uncompahgre Valley and its hot springs, which had belonged to them for generations. It had been agreed that this was to remain part of the Ute reservation. The soil in this valley was fertile, and there was plenty of water, making it ideal for farming. In 1874, bold squatters and land developers began encroaching on the outer edges of the valley, claiming homesteads of 160 acres and building their cabins. Gubernatorial candidate Frederick Pitkin's anti-Ute rhetoric encouraged the squatters, and the loud Ute protests were ignored. Relations between Utes and Coloradans soured even further.

# 8

# The Ninth Cavalry in Colorado, 1875

In September 1875, Colonel Hatch received orders transferring the Ninth Regiment of Buffalo Soldiers from Texas to the Territory of New Mexico. After nine years battling Indians and chasing outlaws in Texas, the Buffalo Soldiers welcomed the transfer to New Mexico Territory, the land of the Apache. They faced plenty of trouble from the rampaging Mescalero and Jicarillo Apaches; Victorio and the Warm Springs Apaches were fighting to remain in their homeland in southwestern New Mexico. In Arizona, Geronimo and his renegades were raiding homesteads, attacking stagecoaches carrying the mail, murdering miners and travelers.

In addition to chasing Apaches, the Buffalo Soldiers were responsible for keeping the peace with the Utes in Colorado. These Indians had large reservations, but there were more problems as settlers established homesteads on their land, and prospectors trespassed in the San Juan Mountains. In 1875, two companies of the Ninth Cavalry were posted at Fort Garland in the San Luis Valley of southern Colorado. They patrolled the Ute reservations and the western part of the territory from the New Mexico border to Wyoming.

The Buffalo Soldiers were capable, seasoned soldiers who could spend days in the saddle, but the regiment was operating at half-strength, and there were not enough troopers. The army had dwindled in size from the 55,000 troops authorized in 1866 to about 25,000 by 1876. Although each cavalry troop could have 100 enlisted men, few units ever reached that number, and troopers were always in short supply.

The Buffalo Soldiers of the Ninth Cavalry rode out of these gates to patrol western Colorado to the Wyoming border. *Courtesy of Tom Williams.*

The army's reenlistment numbers were down due to its inhumane policy of denying all military leave for enlisted men. Many of the Buffalo Soldiers who'd been battling Indians in Texas or the fierce Plains tribes in eastern Colorado never had any military leave. They'd spent five challenging years on the frontier without seeing their families or friends back home. When a Buffalo Soldier's enlistment ended, he thought long and hard before signing up for another five years.

If a soldier was killed or seriously wounded, army policy would not allow him to be replaced by a new recruit. This practice of intentionally decreasing the size of the army by attrition in the midst of the Indian Wars created a severe hardship. Since the Buffalo Soldiers were involved in so many battles on the frontier, their regiments were dangerously depleted by casualties, and small companies of troopers were often greatly outnumbered by large war parties. By the middle of 1876, the Ninth Regiment had only half the number of men for duty that it should have, and General Sheridan complained that there was only one soldier for every 75 square miles.

The Ninth Cavalry troopers were sent to small posts in remote regions of the territory to protect homesteaders, stagecoaches, travel routes, and tiny settlements. When trouble with the Chiricahua Apaches erupted in southern Arizona, Colonel Hatch requested the transfer of two Ninth Cavalry companies, D and L, back from Colorado to help with the fight. General Pope refused, explaining, "They are the only cavalry troops in Colorado!" The army unrealistically expected fewer than 200 Buffalo Soldiers to control several thousand Utes in Colorado; the rest of the Ninth Cavalry battled Victorio in New Mexico and the Chiricahuas in Arizona.

The Buffalo Soldiers in Colorado were led by Captain Francis Dodge, who'd served with the USCT during the Civil War and had developed great respect for the courage and fighting ability of these men. When the Black regiments were authorized by Congress in 1866, Dodge transferred to the Ninth Cavalry, and several of his USCT soldiers quickly enlisted in his new command. He served with these Black troopers in Texas for nine years, fighting Indians and pursuing outlaws, and he was angered by Texans' racism. He appreciated the courage and stamina of his troops and let them know it. They respected Captain Dodge's leadership and humor, and an easy camaraderie born of shared experiences in tough situations developed between them. No other company in the army had a better record for high morale and devotion to duty than his Company D.

The Ninth Cavalry had lost men in battles in Texas, and in February 1876, the regiment's ranks were increased by 91 recruits who received a hearty welcome when they rode into Santa Fe. They were sent to posts scattered around the territory, while 19 new soldiers were assigned to D company. They continued north to Fort Union and then rode on to Fort Garland in southern Colorado.

Captain Dodge was pleased to welcome:

**Madison Ingoman**, an experienced cavalryman who'd fought Indians with the regiment in Texas for seven years. He served in Colorado until 1880, when he returned with this unit to New Mexico Territory. Engaged in frequent battles with the renegades, he earned two citations for bravery against the Apaches in 1881.

**Clinton Greaves**, who'd fought with the Buffalo Soldiers in Texas. After two years in Colorado, he returned to New Mexico when the problems with the Apaches intensified. He received the Medal of Honor for bravery fighting Victorio's renegades in the Florida Mountains in January 1877.

**Private John Q. Adams**, who'd served five years with the Ninth Cavalry's Company C before transferring into Captain Dodge's Company D. An early arrival in New Mexico Territory, he'd seen action against the Apaches. After two years in Colorado, he returned to New Mexico and was cited for bravery against Victorio's Apaches in the Florida Mountains in 1877.

**Sergeant Henry Johnson** had been in the army for 12 years, and this was his third enlistment. Just five feet, five inches tall, Johnson was from Virginia and enlisted in 1867 in the Tenth Cavalry. He fought the Cheyenne on the Republican River in one of the regiment's first battles and was promoted to sergeant in November 1869. He lost his rank in 1871 for a minor infraction but earned his sergeant's stripes again after transferring to the Ninth Cavalry and fighting in Texas. He came west to Fort Union, New Mexico Territory, and joined Dodge's company in Colorado.

**Caleb Benson**, a new recruit for D Company, was sent north to Fort Union with a few other inexperienced soldiers. Orphaned at 14 and uncertain about what to do with his life, Caleb decided to join the army and enlisted in South Carolina in February 1875. Since 21 was the legal age for enlistment, and he had no parents to consent to his actions, Caleb declared, "I am 21 years 7 months of age and know of no impediment to my serving honestly and faithfully as a soldier." The recruiter wasn't overly inquisitive, so Caleb signed his papers with an *X*, and the five foot-four-inch boy who weighed 135 pounds became one of 91 new recruits for the Ninth Cavalry headed for Fort Clark, Texas. Shortly after his arrival in Texas, and still new to riding, Caleb got a taste of frontier army life when his company went on a three-week scouting patrol. The troopers covered 354 miles of rough country, a riding challenge that stretched Caleb's muscles, tested his endurance, made his joints creak, and chafed his backside. When the 91 recruits rode into Santa Fe in May 1876, Caleb, now nearly 16 years old, marveled at the dusty territorial capital that was so different from the South.

The Apaches were causing plenty of trouble in New Mexico, and Caleb had been in a couple of skirmishes by the time he went to Colorado. Coming from the Lowcountry in South Carolina, Caleb was amazed at the snow-covered peaks and big valleys, but he didn't like the frigid winter cold or the deep snowdrifts in the mountains. In the summer of 1877, Caleb was riding with Captain Dodge and the boys of D company, watching for the telltale smoke of wildfires. It was dry, with little rain, and the heat and high winds swept the sunbaked valleys and parched forests that were primed to explode into blazing infernos. Usually, a thunderstorm was welcome, but the summer storms brought a lot of thunder and lightning that started hundreds of wildfires. Ranchers and homesteaders were quick to accuse the Indians when a fire began, but the innocent Utes feared the terrible damage these fires brought to the land and its wildlife as well.

On August 1, 1876, Colorado became the 38th state in the Union, the Centennial State, a cause for giant celebrations. Once the festivities were over, the new state's citizens got busy scheming ways to get the Utes out of Colorado. Frederick Pitkin, a candidate for territorial governor, was a strong supporter of these plans.

During the summer of 1877, the Buffalo Soldiers patrolled South Park, an enormous mountain valley in the Front Range, encompassing over 1,000 miles of land. Then they went farther north to scout in Middle Park and North Park, which were near the White River Agency in northwestern Colorado. Despite long, hard days in the saddle, everyone's morale was high, and the jokes and banter between the troopers made the hours fly. The Utes were surprised when they saw the Buffalo Soldiers for the first time in Middle Park. They wondered about these men with black faces who wore the same blue uniforms as the white soldiers. One Ute, Quinkent, said he'd heard about these men, but this was the first time he'd seen them. "The people thought they were very funny, and they called the Buffalo Soldiers 'Mariacat'z, Black White Men, white men with black faces.'" Most of the Utes did not like the Buffalo Soldiers and sullenly refused to speak when they encountered them along the trail.

In March 1878, when the rations and food arrived at the Los Pinos Agency near the Uncompahgre Reservation, the Utes were angry when they saw their small amount of supplies. Immediately, they demanded that a month's rations be given to them instead of the customary one week's worth. The Indian agent named Weaver was frightened by the Utes' hostility and sent a message to Fort Garland requesting troops to maintain order during distribution of the rations. Lieutenant Valois and Company D rode over the San Juan Mountains and stood by while Weaver distributed the amount demanded by the Utes.

The following month, when the Indians returned to Los Pinos, they again demanded a four-week supply of rations. This time Weaver complied without the presence of troops. On the third month, the Indians repeated their demands, but Weaver refused, told them to leave, and locked up the agency's storehouse. Then he sent to Fort Garland for troops. The angry

Pack train of supplies ready to leave Fort Garland with the Buffalo Soldiers, who spent long days in the saddle on patrol. *Courtesy of History Colorado.*

Utes loitered around the agency and waited several days until the cavalry arrived. Once again, the soldiers stood by as Weaver distributed the supplies, only this time the sullen, grumbling Utes received just one week's worth. Trouble was expected when the angry Utes left the reservation to hunt for game to supplement these rations.

Tensions escalated when trespassing prospectors found placer gold in the LaPlata River on the Southern Ute Reservation. Expanding their search of the Indians' land, they discovered large deposits of gold in quartz rock, which brought hundreds of gold seekers with picks and gold pans in hand, ready to grab their fortunes. The angry Utes protested, and when the Buffalo Soldiers ordered the prospectors to leave, there was a loud uproar. The miners were furious and balked at abandoning their rich claims, so Captain Dodge sent a messenger to Fort Union, requesting additional troops immediately. Major Albert Morrow and four companies of the Ninth Cavalry came and set up their camp on the LaPlata River and were soon joined by Colonel Hatch and Captain A. Kimball with five additional companies of Buffalo Soldiers from Santa Fe and Fort Wingate, New Mexico. This show of armed military force finally convinced the trespassing prospectors that it was in their best interest to look for gold someplace else. They reluctantly left the Ute land,

and the Ninth Cavalry patrolled the LaPlata area for weeks to make sure they didn't return. The angry Utes remained nearby, sinister and menacing, disgusted with the white men and their useless treaties.

This confrontation on the LaPlata River led to a council between Colonel Hatch and Ignacio, the Southern Ute chief, and several of his warriors. They discussed the "Strip," a narrow piece of reservation land along the New Mexico border that had been in contention between the Utes and white settlers for several years. Cattle from ranches on both sides of the Strip often strayed onto this part of the reservation. Each side accused the other of stealing their livestock, and the situation was reaching a boiling point. The ranchers demanded the Southern Utes give up the Strip, significantly decreasing the size of their already small reservation. The Utes angrily refused, but since no agreement was reached, the Strip was ripe for trouble.

In September 1878, Caleb Benson and D Company were attacked by Indians near the mouth of the Mancos River in southwestern Colorado. The soldiers managed to fight off their assailants and get out of the area, but they didn't know if they'd been attacked by Utes or Jicarilla Apaches, who roamed northern New Mexico. During the winter of 1878–79, Captain Dodge and the men of Company D returned to Pagosa Springs in the San Juan Basin west of the Continental Divide. They hoped their presence would keep the Southern Utes on their small reservation. The troops camped near three sulfur hot springs pools that were fed by a deep geothermal hot spring, which the Utes called "Pagosa." This Ute word meant "healing waters with a bad smell," and for generations, they had come to these hot springs to soak their aching bodies and cure their physical ailments.

Caleb Benson, Clint Greaves, and the other troopers built a sawmill here and began cutting trees from the surrounding forests. As quickly as trees were sawed into planks, they were used to construct barracks, which the soldiers hoped to complete before the winter snows began. They knew that at this high altitude, staying warm in canvas tents during a howling blizzard would be impossible. The new post was called Fort Lewis at Pagosa Springs, and Company D spent the winter of 1878–79 there. In the spring when the snow melted, they built a military road through the San Juan Mountains to Fort Garland, making a much shorter route. In September 1878, K Company was detailed to accompany the engineers who were surveying the state's borders between Colorado, New Mexico, and Utah.

While trouble between the whites and the Utes kept the two companies of Buffalo Soldiers busy in Colorado, the other units of the Ninth Regiment had their hands full in New Mexico. When they weren't chasing Apaches or scouting for wandering renegade Kiowas and Comanches, the men repaired the forts, built small houses, or added quarters to the barracks for the Black laundresses, who weren't married to enlisted men. They built a hospital at Fort Stanton in southern New Mexico, where many soldiers who were wounded by Apaches were patients. When wildfires blew up in the tinder dry grassland and forests, the troopers joined homesteaders and ranchers in the fight against these blazing infernos. While they were scouting for Apaches, the troopers mapped a great deal of the New Mexico Territory, which was a big help to the military, settlers, and travelers. Their maps identified mountain ranges, peaks, land elevations, and deadly areas like White Sands. They marked the boundaries of military and Indian reservations and identified travel, mail, and military routes.

In April 1879, Victorio attacked settlers near Silver City, New Mexico, and the Ninth Cavalry spent most of that year chasing his band as they rampaged through the region, then fled to Texas or Mexico. The shortage of troops was so severe that Captain Dodge and D Troop were even sent from Colorado to Fort Bayard, in the southwestern part of New Mexico, to protect terrified settlers. In early fall of 1879, these Buffalo Soldiers returned to Colorado to patrol the Ute reservations, and after several days in the saddle, they reached Fort Garland. That evening, their meal included fresh meat and vegetables from the post garden, a pleasant change from beans and hard tack. They spent a night indoors under the barracks' roof, instead of under the stars rolled in a blanket on the ground. The following morning, they grabbed their boots with the bugler's first notes of "Reveille" and headed for the stable. D Company quickly assembled on the parade ground, and as the trumpeter sounded "Boots and Saddles," they mounted up and were ready to ride.

The Buffalo Soldiers headed north, traveling along the Arkansas River and the spectacular Sangre de Cristo Mountains, their peaks towering over 14,000 feet high. They crossed a pass over the Sawatch Range into South Park and spent days riding through this mountain valley. When they reached Middle Park, there were rumors of Ute unrest at the White River Agency farther north. The new Indian agent, Nathan Meeker, who had taken over in May 1878, had no experience with the Utes and was convinced that they should give up their nomadic life and become farmers. He had shown little interest in trying to understand his charges and had been complaining about the Utes' uncooperative attitude.

White settlers continued to ignore treaties and trespassed on the two Ute reservations. The Utes were understandably angry because they had given up so much of their ancestral lands in Colorado, and the white people kept grabbing more. Persistent prospectors swarmed over the mineral-rich San Juan Mountains, the traditional Ute hunting grounds. The Utes were angry when the treaty violations weren't stopped, and they retaliated by burning settlers' cabins, stealing their livestock, ambushing lone travelers on the trails, and occasionally wounding or killing an interloper. There was a constant undercurrent of anger and resentment boiling just below the surface, and the threat of a Ute uprising in Colorado was real.

# 9

# Meeker's Troubles with the Utes

The Utes were not warlike, and when settlers and prospectors invaded their land, they tried negotiations and treaties to keep peace. When the white people broke the treaties, invaded their hunting grounds, and settled on their land, they grew angry and resentful, but they did not wage endless war to stop the white expansion as the Plains Indians did. The Buffalo Soldiers kept the situation with the Utes under control until 1878, when Nathan Meeker became Indian agent at the White River Agency. This was the beginning of events that culminated in tragedy.

In 1869, Meeker borrowed a large amount of money from Horace Greeley, the newspaper man, to buy land and found the Union Colony in northern Colorado. He named this utopian community, which was based on Christian ideals and an agricultural economy, "Greeley" to honor the man who had inspired him. Desperate for money to repay this debt, Meeker eagerly became the Indian agent at the White River Ute Reservation, although he had no experience with Native Americans.

Meeker didn't respect the Utes or their culture and often spoke of them as "misguided children." He was determined to make the White River Ute settlement into a Christian farming commune, and after enduring a year of his clumsy attempts to transform them into farmers, a revolt of the angry, frustrated Utes became inevitable. In the fall of 1878, Meeker refused to allow the Ute men to leave the reservation to hunt for game for their winter food supply. To make certain the Utes remained at the agency, Meeker distributed the food and rations to only the male head of each

Nathan Meeker, agent at White River, was determined to make the Utes give up their way of life and become farmers. *Courtesy of History Colorado.*

family. He ignored the Ute way of life and said men must work in the fields, though it was traditionally the responsibility of the women. He announced that men who did not spend enough time farming would receive less rations for their families.

Meeker often didn't distribute the food and supplies to the Utes on time. Rations and food supplies were purchased by the government and shipped by rail to the depot at Rawlins, Wyoming, where they were stored in a warehouse and then hauled in freight wagons to the agency. This system was full of problems because government red tape held up purchases, and supplies were often stolen by corrupt contractors. During the harsh winter of 1878–79, Meeker didn't pay the storage cost, so the Ute rations were held in the Rawlins warehouse, and the agency storeroom remained empty. The Utes were hungry, and the men ignored his unreasonable refusal to allow them to hunt and left the reservation anyway.

Meeker's predecessor at White River had started an irrigation project, but he had little luck getting the Indians to dig ditches. When Meeker took over, he encountered stubborn resistance from Utes, who were unwilling to wield shovels or dig in the dirt. They refused to hoe weeds to clear an area for planting, declaring that was "women's work." Meeker's efforts to teach the Utes that farming would provide food to feed their families were ignored. He was dissatisfied with their unwillingness to abandon their nomadic way of life to become farmers, and he wrote letters and articles complaining about his unpleasant experiences at White River. These pieces were published in the *Greeley Tribune*, the newspaper he'd founded eight years earlier, and then reprinted in the Denver papers. As the agent described his futile efforts to persuade the Utes to dig an irrigation ditch or to get rid of their prized race horses, his frustration with them was evident.

The Indian agent's impatience and intolerance of the Utes' ways worried them, but they were most concerned about his frequent communications with newspapers, the military, and numerous government authorities. His constant complaints published in the newspapers increased antagonism toward the Indians, who feared attack or the loss of their reservation land. Meeker continued to browbeat the Utes and then tried to intimidate them with threats to have them arrested, "thrown into chains" and punished by troops from Fort Steele, Wyoming. This infuriated them and contributed to the disaster ahead.

The Utes were the first Indians to acquire horses in the 1600s, and they called themselves the People of the Horse. The White River Utes had many fine animals, well known for their speed and stamina. The size and quality of a man's herd of horses was evidence of his wealth and prestige. The Ute men and boys spent a lot of time training their mounts, trading horses, racing and betting on their fastest animals. The men worked together to construct a safe, firm, race track for their horses. Horse races were traditional at their celebrations and gatherings, and the Utes were always ready to pit their ponies against any white settler who thought he had a fast horse.

Unfortunately, Meeker was determined to get rid of the Utes' horses. He complained to the Commissioner of Indian Affairs that the Indians were "always horse racing, consequently gambling, their main purpose for nine months of the year." He continued, "An Indian without a horse is nobody. Only those young men who have no horses will work....They would rather give up cattle than horses." He was determined to break up the "Ute horse culture to move them closer to civilization." He lectured the men incessantly that "horses take up too much time." The Utes stubbornly guarded their herds, rotating them often through the best pastures at the agency. When Meeker decided to move the agency headquarters from its original site near the mountains to Powell Park by the White River, the Utes objected. This large valley, with its lush grass, was a favorite pasture for their ponies, but Meeker decided it would be a prime location for farming. The fertile soil would produce a lot of crops when it was irrigated, so he became determined to plow up the valley's meadows and build fences around them.

When the Ute men learned of Meeker's plan, they met him and explained the importance of the grassy pasture for their hundreds of ponies. His blunt response was, "Get rid of the horses." Jack, a leading chief, tried to reason with the Indian agent and pointed out that the agency site had been designated by treaty, and no new law had authorized its relocation. He suggested an alternative area that was suitable for farming and even offered to clear the sagebrush and plow it for planting. Meeker stubbornly refused to consider the alternative land, ignored the Utes' anger, and moved the agency to Powell Park. Then he began plowing up its grassy meadows and put the resentful Utes to work digging an irrigation ditch from the nearby White River.

In late 1878, a group of frustrated White River Ute leaders made several trips to the Los Pinos Agency and complained to Chief Ouray about Meeker. They asked the Indian agent there to write to Washington, requesting that Meeker be replaced. They brought samples of the moldy "black flour" that Meeker had distributed to them, which made their children sick. The Los Pinos agent sent the letter and moldy flour to the Commissioner of Indian Affairs as an example of the unsatisfactory conditions at the White River Agency.

When there had been no action from Washington by March 1879, Jack and the Ute leaders went to Denver and asked Governor Pitkin to remove Meeker and replace him with another agent who was more understanding of the Utes' situation. Newly elected governor Pitkin had campaigned relentlessly on the platform "The Utes Must Go!" and was unwilling to do anything to make life easier for them. This anti-Ute governor led local politicians and settlers in their exaggerated claims against these Indians, and he was supported by newspapers that clamored for the complete removal of the Utes from Colorado. The *Boulder News* declared that if the Utes refused to sell their land or leave peacefully, the dispute should "be settled by the force of arms." The *Denver Tribune*, still angry over the army's removal of the miners from the LaPlata River area, raged that "seven hundred hearty pioneers were being prodded out of the country by American bayonets so a small, idle band of nomads could roam over 20 million acres of hunting ground."

Governor Pitkin's secretary and former newspaperman William Vickers, had written many anti-Ute articles for Denver newspapers during the gubernatorial campaign. After Pitkin took office, Vickers continued to pen inflammatory pieces to keep the public stirred up, and Meeker's letters complaining about his Ute charges fueled the fire. Pitkin's antagonism toward the Utes was shared by Henry Teller, one of Colorado's first senators. He was aligned with powerful citizen groups that were looking for any reason to take action against the Indians. Teller loudly opposed Secretary of the Interior Carl Schurz's policies to integrate the Utes peacefully. When Pitkin refused to help, the discouraged Utes returned to White River.

In March 1879, Meeker wrote to Major Thornburgh, the commander at Fort Steele near Rawlins, Wyoming, that the Utes were buying large amounts of ammunition from stores on the Yampa and Snake Rivers. He said they were planning an uprising and demanded that troops come to the agency.

Major Frederick Thornburgh had served in the Civil War and through his political connections had been promoted to major over 250 more qualified captains and lieutenants. He was the youngest major on active duty in 1878, when, at 32, he was put in command of Fort Fred Steele at Rawlins. Thornburgh investigated Meeker's complaints and found that they were exaggerated and untrue.

Tensions between Meeker and the Utes increased, and every time a horse was stolen, game was killed, or small bands of Indians were seen off the reservation, he wrote another letter to Thornburgh. He blamed the Utes for every disturbance and soon began sending telegrams, insisting that troops were required to establish his authority. When Major Thornburgh didn't bring the militia to White River, Meeker angrily telegraphed his supervisor, General Crook, with numerous complaints about the Utes and Thornburgh's failure to act. General Crook ordered yet another investigation, which once again showed that Meeker's complaints were exaggerated. General Crook, who was involved with Apache warfare, angrily told Major Thornburgh to handle Meeker himself.

Although he had little military experience on the frontier, Thornburgh realized the anger and tensions at White River might suddenly explode. Due to congressional underfunding, Fort Steele was seriously undermanned, under-equipped, and unprepared for any engagement with the Utes. There were only three companies of cavalry stationed there, and when Thornburgh requested additional troops, his request was denied because all available soldiers were fighting Victorio in New Mexico.

The Utes had given up much of their land in treaties, but they had retained hunting rights. Settlers complained constantly when Indian hunting parties were in their area, accusing them of stealing horses and setting fires. During the summer of 1878, before the Victorio War began, several hundred troopers of the Ninth Cavalry from Fort Lewis at Pagosa Springs and Fort Garland patrolled Middle and North Parks, reassuring worried settlers. When trouble began with the Apaches in 1879, the troops returned to New Mexico, leaving only Captain Dodge and the Buffalo Soldiers.

That summer was extremely dry, and there were numerous wildfires in Middle and North Parks, which the settlers blamed on the Utes. The drought was severe, and the hot winds contributed to the dangerous conditions. Lightning started some wildfires, but others were due to random sparks from logging activity and ore smelters at the mines. Meeker created a commotion about the wildfires, blamed the Utes, and went to Denver to complain to Governor Pitkin. The governor joined the clamor, writing to the Bureau of Indian Affairs, "Immense forests are burning throughout southwestern Colorado....I am satisfied that there is an organized effort on the part of the Indians to destroy the timber of Colorado!" Then he launched into his favorite refrain, "These savages should be removed to the Indian Territory or New Mexico where they can no longer destroy the finest forest in the state." Next Meeker went to Fort Steele, where he repeated his complaints about the fires and the uncooperative Indians to Thornburgh and again demanded that the major bring troops to the agency to "corral the wayward Utes." When Thornburgh refused, Meeker angrily telegraphed Colonel Hatch, who was busy battling Apaches in New Mexico and simply ignored the Indian agent's demands. Persisting, Meeker wrote to army commanders of the forts scattered throughout southern Wyoming, repeating his complaints and his demands for military help. Again, he was ignored. His letters, telegrams, and querulous messages crossed the desks of Governor Pitkin, Senator Teller, and the Bureau of Indian Affairs. He even wrote to Secretary of War Ramsey and Generals Crook, Sherman, and Pope, demanding that troops be sent to the agency to force the Utes to obey him.

Finally, an exasperated Major Thornburgh and four troops of cavalry rode from Wyoming to investigate Meeker's complaints again. The major talked to settlers around the agency, who said the Utes hadn't committed any depredations or shown any hostility toward them, and one rancher even remarked that he found the Utes "to be peaceful and polite." Thornburgh determined that the fires were most likely due to the "carelessness of white settlers," especially railroad workers cutting ties for the tracks. He reported to his supervisors that he couldn't verify any of Meeker's complaints and said it was obvious that the agent had lost control of the Utes and was angry because they refused to farm.

In late summer of 1879, Meeker blamed a house fire near Steamboat Springs on three Utes: Chinaman, Bennett, and Jack. This was a lie, but the agent spread so many rumors about the Utes that homesteaders talked of abandoning their small ranches and cabins because of the "Ute threat." Once again, Meeker fired off volleys of telegrams to Governor Pitkin, Secretary of the Interior Schurz, the Commissioner of Indian Affairs, and General Pope, who commanded the Department of the Missouri, which included Colorado. When they patrolled the Steamboat Springs area, Captain Dodge and the Buffalo Soldiers found no signs of an imminent Ute uprising.

Meeker had been unable to control the Utes by withholding their rations or threats of the military, so he decided to get rid of their racetrack. He thought if it was gone, the Indians would have to give up their horses and would be more willing to tend cattle and farm. This scheme shows his complete lack of understanding of the Utes and why this ended in a bloody tragedy.

On September 10, 1879, Jack and the other Ute leaders found Meeker poised to attack their prized racetrack with his plow. He refused to listen to their angry objections and announced that plowing would begin the following day. The next morning, the hired plowman had just made the first cuts into the racetrack when a rifle bullet whizzed over his head. Work stopped immediately as the plowman fled, and Meeker summoned the Indian leaders for a conference. Again, he threatened to have them all arrested and imprisoned by the army if they interfered with the destruction of their racetrack. He angrily announced that the plowing would resume the following morning. Then he wrote another letter to the Commissioner of Indian Affairs, assuring him that "plowing will proceed." He added, "This is a bad lot of Indians. They have had free rations so long and have been flattered and petted so much that they think of themselves as lord of all."

When the plowing of the racetrack resumed the following day, the Ute chief, Johnson, approached Meeker in front of his office and demanded that it stop. Meeker snapped back saying that Johnson had too many horses and "should get rid of them, kill them!" Their angry discussion became a

Meeker's request for help brought Major Thornburgh and 175 troops from Fort Steele, Wyoming, to White River Indian Agency in September 1879. *Courtesy of Tom Williams.*

shoving match as Johnson grabbed Meeker by the shoulder and shouted that he should leave White River and be replaced by an agent who was "a good man." Meeker lost his balance and fell, striking his shoulder on a nearby fencepost, and Johnson stormed off.

Meeker got to his feet, dusted himself off, and immediately fired off another letter to Major Thornburgh and sent a telegram to Washington. He declared, "I've been assaulted by a leading chief, Johnson, forced out of my house, injured badly, but was rescued by employees....Life of self, employees, and family not safe; want protection immediately." Meeker said that Johnson had dragged him from his office and thrown him to the ground, injuring his shoulder. Then he sent similar messages to Governor Pitkin and General Pope, asking that "at least 100 soldiers be dispatched," adding, "I feel none of the white people are safe."

Secretary of War Ramsey and General Pope were alarmed by Meeker's account of this Ute assault and quickly approved his requests for troops. General Sherman instructed General Sheridan, who was in Chicago, to "order the nearest military commander to forward troops to White River." Unfortunately, no one in Sheridan's office knew where the White River Agency was located, so it took a couple of days of ludicrous trial and error before the order reached Fort Fred Steele in Wyoming.

# 10

# THE BATTLE OF MILK CREEK, 1879

During the summer of 1879, Meeker's complaints about the Utes had been unrelenting, and military officers dealing with a full-scale Apache war thought his problems were petty. Little attention was paid to his constant, querulous demands, and it was increasingly obvious that this dogmatic man wasn't suited for his position as an Indian agent. His inflexible attitude showed that he was incapable of understanding or dealing with the White River Utes. When his distorted account of the threat on his life finally got the desired response, Major Thornburgh was ordered to take a sufficient number of troops to the White River Agency and arrest the "insubordinate Indian Chiefs and enforce obedience to the requirements of Agent Meeker." He was to hold "the ringleaders as prisoners until an investigation can be held."

Before this order could be put into effect, the major, who was on a hunting trip, had to be located. A messenger from Fort Steele spent two days tracking him and finally found the major's camp about 200 miles from Fort Steele in the Colorado mountains. On September 21, 1879, six days after Meeker's angry encounter with Ute chief Johnson, Major Thornburgh read the telegram ordering him to move quickly to White River. Aware that he lacked sufficient soldiers to handle any trouble with the Utes, he requested additional troops, which were immediately dispatched from Fort Russell at Cheyenne.

Thornburgh hired Charlie Rankin, whose supply trains carried provisions to White River, as a guide, and assembled 33 wagons to carry two troops of infantry, rations for 30 days, ammunition and military supplies, plus the Utes' delayed rations. He included an ambulance, a herd of extra horses and mules, and even a sutler's wagon carrying goods and sundries that the soldiers could purchase. On September 22, 1879, Thornburgh, with three companies of the Fifth and Third Cavalry and one infantry company, a force of about 191 enlisted men and officers, left Fort Steele and headed south toward Colorado.

The large column moved slowly, averaging 20 to 25 miles a day, stopping hourly to rest the horses, as they'd done on practice scouting exercises. The young major had no experience fighting Indians and lightheartedly led his equally inexperienced troops across the rolling sagebrush hills into Colorado. The men were in good spirits and optimistic about the outcome of this expedition, which most regarded as just a pleasant excursion. Thornburgh brought his fishing rod in hopes of catching a trophy trout in the Yampa River, plus a bottle of witch hazel to repel mosquitoes. He'd tucked his small leather-covered Bible, a bottle of gin and lemon extract, a box of cigars, and even a framed photograph of his wife into his pack. Young Lieutenant Cherry, a recent West Point graduate, brought his pet greyhound in case there'd be time for hunting; Lieutenant Price, who was in charge of the infantry, was keeping a sharp eye out for burrowing owls, which he was collecting for the Smithsonian.

Thornburgh had included a medical doctor, but he'd decided not to bring the twelve-pound howitzer or a Hotchkiss "mountain gun." These deadly weapons had quickly ended the charges of many Indian war parties on the plains, but Thornburgh expected this to be a simple, uncomplicated police action and did not think these weapons would be needed. The only soldier with experience fighting Indians was Captain Lawson, a 60-year-old Civil War veteran, who was leading a cavalry company. He'd fought all over the West, but none of his men had any combat experience. Lieutenant Price and his infantry troops had spent all of their time in garrison duty and hadn't been in any battles with Indians. Captain Payne, who was in charge of the cavalry units from Fort Russell, had been in just two small skirmishes with Indians.

Finding enough forage for the 370 head of horses and mules was a daily challenge, and after four days, Thornburgh realized they were still only halfway to White River. To hasten their progress, he left part of the supply train at an easily defended spot on Fortification Creek with an infantry company to guard it. The following day, September 26, the troops crossed the Yampa River, and Lieutenant Cherry and guide Charlie Rankin visited a nearby store–trading post, where they learned that Utes from the agency had recently purchased 10,000 rounds of ammunition. The lieutenant was approached by the Ute leader Jack and several others, who asked for a meeting with Major Thornburgh. They accompanied Lieutenant Cherry back to camp, where the major greeted them and offered everyone a cigar. While they were enjoying a friendly smoke, Thornburgh explained his orders to restore the peace and arrest the "troublemakers that Meeker accused of starting fires." The Utes assured him that there was no trouble at the agency and insisted that soldiers weren't needed. Jack angrily said that Meeker was a bad agent and had caused trouble by plowing up the Utes' horse pasture and racetrack, withholding their rations, and accusing them of starting fires. He pointed out that Meeker's lies and frequent threats to have them arrested, put in shackles and chains, and thrown into jail had frightened everyone and added to their distrust. Then Jack warned Thornburgh that if he entered the reservation with his troops, it would be a violation of the treaty of 1868. The Utes would consider it an attack, and there would be trouble. Jack suggested that the major and five officers come alone to the agency to meet Meeker and discuss his problems; the troops remained several miles behind. Thornburgh agreed to consider Jack's suggestion.

Unfortunately, the inexperienced major thought troops on the Utes' land would make them more cooperative. He did not understand the long-lasting impact of the Sand Creek Massacre or how the presence of armed troops aroused the fear and distrust of Indians. He seemed unaware that the Utes were still very angry because Meeker had called for the military, but he decided to follow their suggestion and take just a few officers with him to meet the agent at White River. He sent Meeker a message that his troops would remain behind and would not enter the Ute reservation. That evening, September 27, Colorow, another White River Ute leader, and ten sub-chiefs rode into the army camp and once again confronted Thornburgh about the presence of troops. The major told them, just as he'd told Jack, that he was only coming to arrest three Indians who Meeker had named as "troublemakers."

On the morning of September 28, as Thornburgh and the troops advanced cautiously toward the agency, they overtook a supply wagon hauling a threshing machine for the White River Agency. The driver said he had encountered Colorow, who'd warned him if the soldiers came onto the reservation, the Utes would fight. Then he gave Thornburgh several drawings he'd found scattered about, which pictured the wagon road to White River littered with the bullet-riddled bodies of fallen troopers. The

*Above*: Milk Creek Battlefield Park in Moffat County, Colorado, is in a brush-lined canyon twenty miles northeast of Meeker. The battlefield looks as it did in 1879. *Courtesy of Tom Williams.*

*Left*: Colorow, White River Ute chief, was the leader at the Battle of Milk Creek. He favored war over compromise and often disagreed with Ouray and other leaders. *Public domain, https://americanantiquarian.org*

major said little as he stuffed the ominous drawings into his pocket. That evening, a messenger from the agency arrived at Thornburgh's camp and reported that the Ute women and children had hurriedly taken down their tipis, packed all their goods, and left. There were only 4 tipis at the agency, where there had been 94 the day before. The messenger said Ute leaders, Douglas and Jack, had sent their families to the mountains for their safety, and the men had held war dances the past two nights—all ominous indications of coming trouble.

September 29, 1879, dawned clear and cool with a light dusting of snow on the ground. The troops were on the march early, and their long line twisted like a snake through the valley toward Milk Creek. Thornburgh had changed his mind that morning, disregarded all of the warnings, and decided to take his men onto the Ute reservation. He sent a messenger to Meeker saying that he was bringing his "entire command to within striking distance of your agency." He was certain that Meeker would warn him if there was any real danger.

Milk Creek marked the boundary of the reservation and was about 25 miles from the agency. Although the stream was almost dry, with only a few pools of water scattered among the rocks, Thornburgh ordered a halt so the troops could water their horses. Then he sent Lieutenant Cherry, the scout Joe Rankin, and five troopers ahead to cross the creek and enter the Ute reservation. He left the supply wagons, ambulance, and sutler's cart on a small, open knoll and followed the others across Milk Creek. Clouds of dust rose above their procession as it wound along the agency road past the bluffs of a long, plateau-like mountain with slopes covered with thick Gambel oak.

Lieutenant Cherry and his men were a short distance ahead of Thornburgh and the troops when he was startled to see about 50 mounted Utes watching from a nearby ridge. His alarm increased when he noticed more Indians, armed with rifles, on the bluffs and hidden among the rocks and sagebrush on the hillside ahead. The lieutenant turned in his saddle and waved his hat in Thornburgh's direction. Suddenly, a gunshot broke the silence, and both sides began firing. Who fired that first shot? It's unknown, but the battle was on.

The five cavalrymen with Lieutenant Cherry whirled around to race back toward the wagons, but the Utes quickly picked off their horses with their Henry repeating rifles and .44-caliber Winchesters. At a range of 400 yards, they killed two soldiers and wounded three others. Thornburgh ordered his cavalry troops to retreat and turned back to organize the wagons for defense. He galloped down the road as bullets whizzed around him, and he had just crossed Milk Creek when he was hit in the head by a Ute sharpshooter. Thornburgh fell from his saddle about 500 yards from the supply wagons, dead before he hit the ground.

As deadly gunfire rained down on them from the bluffs, Lieutenant Cherry, Joe Rankin, and two troops of cavalry retreated rapidly to the wagons, carrying and dragging their wounded and dead comrades. Captain Payne, who'd been shot in the arm, took charge, ordering the men to pull the wagons into a circle and then to dig protective rifle pits with their cups, spoons, and bare hands. They carried the wounded to the center of the wagon enclosure and dug a large protective pit around them to serve as the hospital. As the Utes continued firing from the surrounding bluffs, more than 150 soldiers tried to find cover for themselves and their 153 mules and 186 horses. They were crowded into a space that was about 225 feet across and 75 feet deep. The Utes' aim was deadly, and their Winchester repeating rifles and the latest models of Sharps, Henry, and Remington fired more quickly and had greater range than the cavalry's .45-.70 Springfield carbines. Although they were outnumbered, the Utes had the advantage of their high ground positions, and they controlled the battlefield and the small Milk Creek Valley. Just a few hours after the battle began, Douglas, another chief, sent a messenger to the Utes at the White River Agency. When the Indians there learned that troops had crossed onto the Ute lands and were now under attack, the slaughter at the agency began.

The battle at Milk Creek raged all day as the soldiers endured unrelenting gunfire from the front, both flanks, and above. Then the Utes targeted the horses, shooting just to wound the animals. The injured creatures lunged about, screaming and kicking, breaking their tie ropes, and racing frantically around the wagon enclosure, staggering through the trenches, and stumbling into the soldiers. Seeing these suffering, wounded animals was especially painful for the cavalrymen, who loved and valued their horses. They relied on these animals, who were much more than transportation, and many horses were well-loved companions and pets. A Ute later described the chaotic scene: "Soon the space inside the wagon circle was like a burning ants' nest, with horses, kicking, screaming, plunging, and rolling all over the place." The Utes, who were avid horsemen and loved their own ponies, later said they disliked shooting the cavalry's animals, and that "everyone was glad when there were no more animals to be shot" because all of the army's faithful horses and mules lay dead.

Without their horses, the troopers were trapped with no means of escape. Dust and gun smoke hung over Milk Creek until midafternoon, when a cold, steady wind that smelled like snow began to blow. Then the Utes stealthily approached the wagons and set the nearby dry grass on fire in an attempt to burn up the troopers' only protection. Soon, a thin spiral of smoke twisted upward from one wagon as the fire, pushed by the wind, grew rapidly. Yelling an alarm, the soldiers rushed to fight the flames, beating at them with burlap bags, blankets, and even their own shirts. Frantically, they gathered handfuls of dirt to throw on the flames as an eight-foot-high wall of fire raced toward the other wagons. A sergeant dashed out and managed to set a backfire in the tall grass and sagebrush, but the blaze chased him back and swept into the barricade, setting the canvas tops of the wagons on fire. A trooper managed to pull the burning tops off some of the wagons, saving them from incineration.

The dancing flames lit up the enclosed area, making it easy for the Utes to pick off even more troopers as they pulled the burning wagons away from the protective circle. The fire destroyed several wagons that were outside the barricade and burned up all of the supplies they contained. Five more soldiers were killed while firefighting, and twelve were wounded. Dr. Robert Grimes of Fort Laramie tended the growing number of injured, moving from one to another as bullets whizzed around him. When he opened a medicine chest to get a bandage, he was shot in the left shoulder, but after receiving medical attention himself, the doctor resumed his rounds, caring for men who were in worse condition.

That night, under the cover of darkness, the troopers dragged the dead horses and mules out of the enclosure and piled up their carcasses to form a protective breastwork in front of the wagons. Then Dr. Grimes directed them to roll the dead men in canvas shrouds and add their bodies to the reinforcements. They hurriedly unloaded the supply wagons that hadn't burned and stacked the barrels, boxes, bedding, kegs, bags of flour and cornmeal on top of the horse carcasses to make the protective wall higher. Since the wounded were in dire need of water, two soldiers tried to cross the open area to Milk Creek to fill their canteens, but they were quickly picked off by the sharp-eyed Utes.

Captain Payne had 96 unwounded men against 200 to 300 Utes, who were strategically placed high in the rocky bluffs on both sides of the small canyon. The troops were pinned down, and advancing forward toward the agency or retreating backward was impossible. Captain Payne could not move his men without horses, and most of their supplies had been burned or destroyed. The Utes had plenty of food, water, and ammunition and could wait them out. He knew that if they did not get reinforcements within the next few days, they would be overrun by the Indians. Payne asked for volunteers to carry dispatches to Captain Dodge with the Buffalo Soldiers, who were on patrol somewhere in these mountains. Another messenger was to try to get through to the telegraph office in Rawlins and send a message to General Crook requesting help. The third messenger was to order the lieutenant, who was guarding the remaining supply wagons, to remain at Fortification Creek.

Joe Rankin and the teamster, John Gordon, volunteered and were joined by two Fifth Cavalry privates. Payne told them bluntly that it was unlikely that all of them would get through, but each man was determined to make the effort. They selected the strongest surviving horses and quietly left the enclosure around midnight. They followed Milk Creek up the valley and then each took a different direction to get through the Ute lines. A full moon bathed the area in silvery light, and the troopers trapped by Milk Creek held their breaths, fearing the messengers would be spotted. For over an hour, they listened for gunfire, which meant someone had been seen, but no sound came. Now Payne and the others had a little hope. Lookouts were posted around the enclosure to keep watch during the night.

The morning of September 30 brought warm sunshine, the groans of the dying, the agonizing cries of the wounded, and more Ute bullets from the surrounding bluffs. Every time there was a break in the gunfire, the soldiers scrambled to haul more horse carcasses from the enclosure to the barricade wall. Groups of weary men huddled in the trenches and tried not to become an Ute sharpshooter's target. The few veteran troopers, who'd fought in the Sioux campaign, crouched next to green recruits who'd never been in a fight before; everyone wondered if any of the messengers had delivered Payne's dispatches.

Early that morning, messenger Joe Rankin reached Fortification Creek, gave the warning, saddled a fresh horse, and rode on. He changed horses at a ranch on the Little Snake River and galloped north through the afternoon and night. At about 2:00 a.m. on Wednesday, October 1, 1879, Rankin rode wearily into Rawlins, Wyoming. As he trotted up Front Street along the railroad tracks to wake the telegraph operator, he thought about the men at Milk Creek. He'd ridden 160 miles to Rawlins in 27 and a half hours to send a telegram to General Crook. Once that was done, Joe found a room, went to bed, and slept.

On October 1, Colonel Wesley Merritt, commander of Fort Russell near Cheyenne, was sick in bed when a telegram came from General Crook at 4:30 a.m., ordering him to take four companies of the Fifth Cavalry, about

234 men with 20 officers, to Rawlins immediately. He'd be joined there by additional troops, and then they were to hurry to the aid of the men at Milk Creek. Tossing aside his blankets, Merritt quickly ordered the troops to be ready with their horses. They assembled provisions and boarded the Union Pacific, leaving Cheyenne that evening. When they arrived in Rawlins, Merritt's troops joined 150 additional soldiers from three companies of the Fourth Infantry from Fort Laramie. In expectation of a major war with the Utes, General Sheridan had ordered 2,000 additional troops from the Department of the Missouri to be ready for transfer to Colorado.

That same day, October 1, a messenger brought news about the events at White River to the Utes at Milk Creek. They knew Chief Douglas and his band had left the agency, and Jack worried that the massacre and this attack at Milk Creek would bring lasting punishment to the Utes. He remembered his railroad journey to Washington, D.C., with Ouray when the treaties were being developed, and he had seen the power of the white people firsthand. Like Ouray, Jack didn't believe the Utes could win a long struggle against the whites, and he was certain retribution would come for this attack on U.S. troops. He was afraid that the White River Utes might be forced off their reservation.

Colorow, whose men had been the first to fire on Lieutenant Cherry, was certain that the Utes had taught the white men a lesson. He laughed as the smell of decaying horse flesh drifted toward the bluffs where the Utes were entrenched. Colorow foolishly thought that he could force the soldiers to abandon their barricade, saying, "The bad smell will bring many flies—big, fat, blue flies. Those flies will get even fatter on those dead horses, and when the soldiers run out of food, they can roast them." He didn't know that the U.S. troops' call for help had been received, and aid would be coming if the soldiers could just hold on.

While Colonel Merritt was getting his forces ready for the march to Milk Creek, the other couriers were trying to locate Captain Dodge and the Buffalo Soldiers. They alerted everyone they met about the battle with the Utes at Milk Creek, causing a great deal of alarm among the ranchers and settlers. Dodge and his troop of Buffalo Soldiers had been patrolling Middle Park all summer and had orders to rush to Meeker's aid whenever he needed it. However, the Indian agent had made so many unverified complaints about the Utes that Dodge shared the skepticism about the seriousness of his troubles. A few days earlier, Captain Dodge had visited the store–trading post near the reservation, a favorite of the Utes for bartering and a good place to pick up agency news. The storekeeper hadn't heard of any trouble with the Indians, while the mail carrier, who made regular deliveries there, assured Dodge that "all was sweetness at the agency," and everything had been smoothed over between Meeker and Johnson.

Dodge and his men returned to Middle Park, where they received a series of conflicting orders that had them galloping to Meeker's aid until they were intercepted by another messenger with orders to turn back. This ridiculous situation reflected the turmoil that Meeker had created ever since he took over as the Indian agent at White River. A third courier brought new orders from General Sheridan, which indicated that Meeker's litany of complaints had finally gotten the desired results: a large number of troops commanded by Major Thornburgh were headed toward the White River Agency to settle problems with the Utes. Captain Dodge and his Buffalo Soldiers were not needed, and Sheridan ordered them to return to Middle Park to continue their patrols. This chaos of conflicting orders brought plenty of chuckles from the Black soldiers, while an exasperated Captain Dodge marveled at their good humor while they were dashing back and forth.

In stark contrast to Sheridan's assumption that the situation at the White River Agency would soon be under control, and while Dodge and his troops were galloping around, help was desperately needed at Milk Creek. The courier sent by Captain Payne was frantically trying to track down the Buffalo Soldiers, whose whereabouts changed with their constantly changing orders. The messenger alerted settlers living near the Yampa River about the Ute ambush and the troopers' dire situation. Afraid the Indians were going on a rampage, most settlers grabbed a few belongings and fled down the Yampa River. One cool-headed rancher took the time to write a note to Captain Dodge on a large piece of paper. He tied it firmly to a bush along the trail, and amazingly, on September 30, the Buffalo Soldiers found that note. It read, "Hurry up! Thornburgh killed! The troops have been defeated. (signed) E.C.C." This was especially alarming because Dodge didn't know the whereabouts of Thornburgh's troops.

Then on October 1, Captain Dodge had a stroke of good luck when the third messenger from Milk Creek finally tracked him down. He delivered Captain Payne's call for help and offered to lead Dodge and his 35 Buffalo Soldiers to the besieged troops. The captain gave his men a quick briefing, outlining the danger ahead, and the huge odds against them. These Buffalo Soldiers had been in plenty of tough situations before, and they were ready for the fight. Every man was issued rations for several days and 250 rounds of ammunition before they set out at a brisk pace. They sang songs and joked as they rode through the chill, dark night, hoping to reach Milk Creek before dawn. They passed the two burned freight wagons that had been hauling goods and supplies to the agency. The bodies of the two teamsters lay sprawled in the dust, hacked and mutilated.

Captain Dodge and D Company reached Milk Creek just before dawn on October 2, thankful that they were still concealed by darkness. They had ridden 70 miles in 23 hours, which was very fast time. As the Buffalo Soldiers approached the troopers' enclosure, they expected the Utes to start firing, but surprisingly, only the muffled sounds of their horses' hooves broke the stillness. They were challenged by the sentry in the barricade, who recognized the messenger's voice. The Buffalo Soldiers were greeted with shouts of joy and gratitude by the exhausted troops, and there was plenty of backslapping and relieved grins all around. Captain Payne and 42 of his men were wounded, and the rest were in pitiful condition—dehydrated from lack of water and exhausted from too much sun and mental strain. Most hadn't slept, and they were sickened by the nauseating stench, which made it difficult to breathe.

One Fifth cavalryman described the arrival of the Buffalo Soldiers in the October 25, 1879 *Army Navy Journal*, "We were getting pretty da— tired. It was the third morning after we were corralled and…we didn't know whether any of our messengers had struck help or not.…When Captain Dodge came up at a canter leading the rest of his men…we forgot all about the danger of exposing ourselves and leaped up out of the pits to shake hands all around. Why we took those darkies in right along with us in the pits. We let 'em sleep with us and they took their knives and cut off strips of bacon from the same sides we did."

The Utes had watched Captain Dodge and his men quietly enter the enclosure, and for an unknown reason, they had held their fire. Unfortunately, this cease-fire was temporary, and Dodge and his troops had barely reached the trenches when the Indians began shooting. Just as they had before, the Ute sharpshooters took aim at the Buffalo Soldiers' horses first, making the Black soldiers endure the sight of their faithful mounts dropping right and left. The terrible screams of the animals rent the air, and the furious troopers returned the Utes' gunfire with a vengeance. One injured animal fell into the hospital pit, landing in the midst of 40 wounded men, and only the quick action of the Black troopers, who managed to drag the horse away, saved them from being trampled. In just a short time, all but four of Company D's horses were victims of the Indian sharpshooters. The remaining animals were wounded and screaming in pain.

With daylight, the Utes saw that these new arrivals were the "soldiers with black faces," and the Indians watched them with interest. One said that the sudden appearance of these Buffalo Soldiers was "something to wonder about and to laugh about—perhaps sometimes to be a little angry about…but nothing to be afraid of." Many Utes didn't like the Black troops and felt their presence was an insult. They hopped around and made-up words to songs that mocked the men with black faces. They called out taunts, "Mariacat'z! The black white men! The Buffalo Soldiers!" Then they'd sing:

*You Soldiers with black faces!*
*You rode into battle behind the white soldiers;*
*But you can't take off your black faces*
*And the white faced-soldiers make you ride behind them!*

When a group of Buffalo Soldiers came out of the enclosure carrying shovels, the Utes began waving their arms and shouting, but the Black men acted like they didn't hear. They ignored the Indians as they shoveled dirt over the dead horses and dug additional rifle trenches. The Indians took a few random shots at them and then just watched. Dodge and Payne discussed the possibility of attacking the Utes, but the Buffalo Soldiers, despite their willingness to fight, were greatly outnumbered, and the enemy's superior position on the bluffs made this impractical. Payne's troops were greatly encouraged by their arrival because the Utes' siege had been broken, and

Sergeant Henry Johnson braved Ute gunfire and dashed across an open area to get water from Milk Creek for wounded soldiers. He was awarded the Medal of Honor. *Courtesy of National Archives.*

hopefully, more help would be coming soon. The grizzled veteran, Captain Lawson, took this occasion to make a speech praising the bravery of everyone and concluded with, "You men of the 9th Cavalry are the whitest Black men I have ever seen!"

That night, the Buffalo Soldiers tackled the dismal job of dragging the carcasses of their precious horses to the breastwork and piling them up. Despite their use in the barricade, more than 300 dead animals still lay between the troops and Milk Creek, filling the air with the horrible stench of their rotting carcasses. The Black soldiers finished digging the trench in front of the barricade, while the Indians' well-aimed rifle fire had them jumping in and out of it. Then Dodge positioned his sharpshooters in front, where they had a better chance of picking off the Utes on the bluffs.

For the next four days, the Utes continued the siege, greeting the rising sun every morning with salvos of gunfire, which drove off flocks of buzzards, crows, and coyotes feasting on the carcasses. "The Utes always bring their guns into play just as the boys are stirring about and preparing for breakfast," grumbled a weary soldier. Since they couldn't risk fires for cooking, cold rations were the order of the day, so the Buffalo Soldiers shared theirs with the white troopers. Their canteens of water provided much-needed relief to the wounded. Unfortunately, these canteens were soon empty, and getting more water was a problem for everyone. The creek was about 200 yards from the barricade, but venturing out with a canteen or bucket was likely to bring death from the Utes' brutal barrage of gunfire. If a head popped up to take a look around or there was movement in the enclosure, it quickly brought a whizzing bullet.

On October 4, under the cover of darkness, Sergeant Henry Johnson, who supervised the Buffalo Soldiers, crouched down in the forward rifle pits and completed his nightly rounds under heavy gunfire. Then he grabbed as many canteens as possible and sprinted 200 yards across open ground to the creek. The Utes continued firing at him, and despite the bullets buzzing around his head like angry bees, Johnson was miraculously unscathed. He quickly filled all the canteens and raced back to his thirsty comrades. This water was life-saving for the wounded and gave the exhausted troopers a bit of comfort and hope. Several years later, in 1890, Sergeant Johnson was awarded the Medal of Honor for his bravery at Milk Creek.

Trying to move around was very dangerous and drew volleys of bullets from the Utes. Occasionally, someone was hit and dragged to the hospital pit, where the exhausted doctor tended their wounds. As the grim days dragged on, there was one question in the minds of these worn-out men: Did the other messengers get through? Were troops coming to their rescue? The soldiers tried to create diversions to distract their companions from the misery of their situation. They were simply too exhausted to remain in constant fear and welcomed jokes and funny stories. Several Buffalo Soldiers sang ballads and recited old tales; a group of Black and white soldiers sharing a trench debated and argued about every subject imaginable, like a high school debating society. Most soldiers craved the comfort of a cup of hot coffee to end another miserable day, but this was impossible without a fire. One evening when this desire was stronger than their fear of Ute snipers, several soldiers ventured out to gather sagebrush for a fire to make coffee. They'd spotted several large bushes nearby and succeeded in dragging them back and got a fire going. The aroma of fresh coffee briefly overcame the stench, but there was more gunfire that night than any other during the siege. However, no one ended up in the hospital pit.

The besieged troops at Milk Creek did not know that on October 2, Colonel Merritt and his troops were on the train pulling into the Rawlins depot. From there, 200 men of the Fifth Cavalry quickly unloaded their horses, saddled up, and made ready for the ride south as 150 infantry men piled into wagons. Merritt and his troops set off at a brisk pace for Milk Creek. They moved rapidly, traveling 170 miles in three days, covering the last 70 miles in 20 hours and riding through the night to reach Milk Creek around 5:00 a.m. on October 5.

When Ouray learned about the attack and siege at Milk Creek, he sent a messenger to Jack and the other White River chiefs there, ordering them to "cease hostilities" and "to injure no innocent person." He warned, "Further warfare with the whites will ultimately end in disaster to all parties." Although Ouray had little authority over any of the White River Utes, he was respected and influential. After some discussion, Jack and the other chiefs decided that they had inflicted enough casualties on the army, and if they continued fighting, there was a good chance they themselves would suffer additional losses.

Instead of waking to the usual barrage of gunfire, on October 5, the besieged troopers at Milk Creek heard the notes of a bugle sounding "Officer's Call." Within seconds, every trooper was awake, rifle ready, crouched behind the stinking barricade. When Colonel Merritt and his troops rode into Milk Creek, they faced no opposition because the Utes had vanished, headed for the mountains, ending one of the longest Indian battles in history. As the line of troops came into view, there were shouts of joy and gratitude. Captain Payne limped up to Colonel Merritt and threw his arms around him, exclaiming, "It's a miracle anyone is still alive!"

Merritt was appalled by the condition of the survivors, and one officer said, "The sight was one of the most affecting I have ever seen. Grown men shed tears." Wounded men who were able to walk shambled and limped around the enclosure, stunned by their rescue. Soldiers with the most severe wounds tossed and moaned in the hospital trench, praying for release. Everyone agreed that without the help of the Buffalo Soldiers, Payne and his exhausted troops would have met the same fate as Custer's troops at the Little Big Horn three years earlier. Captain Dodge later praised the

Buffalo Soldiers, saying, "They endured loss of sleep, lack of food, and the deprivations attendant upon their situation without a murmur."

Merritt's men quickly went to work, tending the injured, cleaning and dressing their wounds, and then moving them to tents set up away from the foul-smelling enclosure. Later, the wounded were carefully loaded into the ambulance and wagons for the trip back to Wyoming. The dead troopers were buried at the battle site, and their graves were marked; other crews handled the unpleasant task of covering the dead horses with dirt and rocks.

Captain Payne was the first to lead his weary men north and away from Milk Creek, escorted by Captain Dodge and the Buffalo Soldiers, who were riding borrowed horses. In the six-day battle, 17 troopers, including Major Thornburgh, lost their lives, and 44 soldiers were wounded. The major's body, riddled with bullets, mutilated, and scalped, was taken back to Rawlins to be sent to Omaha for burial. At least 19 Ute Indians had been killed, although some estimates were as high as 37.

When Captain Payne and his troops reached Rawlins on October 19, they wearily climbed aboard the train for the trip back to their post. Captain Dodge and the Buffalo Soldiers rode into Fort Fred Steele, escorted by two welcoming columns of cavalrymen. They were greeted with loud cheers by the waiting crowd. Captain Dodge dismounted and crisply saluted the fort commander as the crowd applauded enthusiastically. Then the Buffalo Soldiers, sitting erect in their saddles, saluted, swept off their campaign hats with a flourish, and bowed to the crowd. This was one of the few times in the West when the Buffalo Soldiers received public recognition from white military authorities for their actions.

Later that day, the Buffalo Soldiers boarded the train for their long journey south to Fort Union, New Mexico. The train stopped in Denver, where a huge crowd and a festive celebration awaited them. Governor Pitkin and city dignitaries welcomed the soldiers at Union Station with speeches praising their bravery, and then the Black troopers led a triumphant parade to the YMCA building. A crowd of both white and Black citizens cheered and clapped as Denver's only Black band broke into a spirited rendition of "When Johnny Comes Marching Home." There were more congratulatory speeches, and the crowd gave a tremendous cheer when Sergeant Henry Johnson stepped up on the stage to tell how "his brave brothers made the most wonderful march on record." He said that even though they were outnumbered by hundreds of Indians, and all their horses had been shot, "not a man was scared." Sergeant John Olney talked about their galloping dash to Milk Creek and how the appearance of the Buffalo Soldiers buoyed

Company D Ninth Cavalry received a heroes' welcome in Denver after the battle at Milk Creek. They rode the train to Alamosa and on to New Mexico Territory. *Courtesy of Tom Williams.*

the spirits of the wounded soldiers and cheered the demoralized white troopers. Caleb Benson delighted the crowds with his story about sharing his rations with the starving white troops. He said the Utes laughed and made fun of them, jeering and calling the Buffalo Soldiers, "white soldiers with black faces—the Mariacat'z!"

A *Rocky Mountain News* reporter wrote, "Other Buffalo Soldiers thrilled the audience with their accounts of fighting Comanches in Texas and Apaches in New Mexico in a very enthusiastic manner. Then everyone turned their attention to the tables loaded with plenty of 'eatables' and enjoyed a splendid feast." Late in the evening, worn out and pleased by all the praise and stuffed with food, the Buffalo Soldiers returned to the depot and boarded the train headed south to New Mexico.

At Milk Creek, Colonel Merritt's troops were reinforced by 900 additional soldiers of the Seventh Infantry from Dakota Territory. They were prepared to quell a major uprising of the Colorado Utes, if necessary. On Saturday, October 11, 1879, Colonel Merritt led the cavalry 25 miles up the road to the White River Agency.

# 11

# THE MEEKER MASSACRE, 1879

Indian Agent Nathan Meeker began the day of September 29, 1879, by lying. He assured Chief Douglas that Major Thornburgh's troops were not going to enter the White River Reservation, although he knew this wasn't true. He had received a message from Thornburgh the previous day saying that he'd changed his plans and was going to bring his troops onto Ute land near the agency.

The Utes had held a war dance the previous night, but Meeker had paid little attention because he knew troops were finally coming. He was certain that the military presence would force the Utes to cooperate with him. Unfortunately, neither the agent nor Thornburgh understood the fear the Utes had of the military or recognized their horrible memories of the Sand Creek Massacre. He misjudged the Indians' anger and didn't warn Major Thornburgh that they had threatened to fight if troops entered their reservation. Meeker's lies put his family, the agency employees, and the approaching soldiers in danger.

It was early afternoon on September 29 when a Ute galloped into White River and began talking excitedly with Douglas and the other Indians. Within the hour, more than 20 Utes grabbed their rifles and suddenly began shooting the agency employees. One by one, the hired hands were killed, and then the Indians broke into the storehouse where the food and rations were kept. They grabbed sacks of flour and sugar, tinned goods, and blankets, and began stacking them in piles.

When Arvilla Meeker, the agent's wife, and their 16-year-old daughter, Josephine, heard the gunshots, they ran into the house and hid under the bed. Flora Price, the blacksmith's wife, and her two young children crawled under, too. The women cowered there, terrified, until they smelled smoke. Frank Dresser, a curly-haired youth who'd been working at the agency only a few months, ran in and rushed them out of the house, which the Utes had set on fire. They ran to the nearby milk house and hid there all afternoon, frightened by the Indians' angry shouts and the occasional gunshots. When the Utes put the torch to the agency buildings, the smoke drifting into the milk house made it very difficult to breathe. They ran out of the milk house and headed for the fields but were seen by the Utes, who shot Frank. Arvilla Meeker couldn't run well due to an old leg injury, and when a bullet grazed her hip, she fell and was the first to be captured. Yelling and shouting, the Utes easily caught Josephine and Flora next. The women were herded to the agency storehouse, where they cowered as the Indians packed the blankets and supplies on mules. Then they rounded up the agency horses and cattle for the journey to the Ute camp in the mountains.

By nightfall on September 29, every agency building was in flames, Nathan Meeker and all of his employees lay dead, their bodies stripped, and some had been hacked, mutilated, burned, and scalped. The two freighters, who brought supply wagons to the agency, died with the rest. The tragedy at the White River Agency had taken place just a few hours after the first shots were fired at Milk Creek. September 29, 1879, a sparkling fall day, that began with optimism and a lie, ended in death and destruction.

The captive women and children were loaded on horses, including frail Arvilla, who had never ridden a horse before. She cried out in pain when Johnson piled her on a raw-boned nag without a saddle. When the caravan rode out of the agency that evening, the captive women were shocked to see its total destruction. Some of the buildings were still smoldering, and the area was littered with smashed farming implements, broken tools, and plundered supplies that had been damaged, ripped open, and tossed about. Choking down her tears, Josephine followed a younger Ute man, Persune, and his two wives; Arvilla, Flora Price, and her two children were herded along the trail by Johnson. Soon, Arvilla was crying from the painful wound in her hip, but Josephine's pleas to let her mother walk were ignored.

While these White River Utes hurried into the mountains, Ouray ordered the Uncompahgre Utes to stay on their reservation on the Western Slope of the Rockies. Ignacio and the Southern Utes remained on their land in southwestern Colorado. The White River renegades would receive no help from the other Utes because they feared the consequences of the attacks on the troops at Milk River and the killings at the agency.

Jack and the others kept a close watch on their captives as they rode across the sagebrush hills and high plateaus, until they crossed the Colorado River. After several days of riding, they stopped on Grand Mesa, west of the Continental Divide, and the three chiefs set up separate camps to keep the captives apart.

A few days later, a group of braves who'd been fighting at Milk Creek rode into the camp where Josephine was being held. These Utes were in great spirits, and they bragged about surprising the cavalry when they'd crossed onto the reservation. They said these soldiers had been trapped and pinned down by Ute gunfire. They laughed about shooting the soldiers' horses and said they'd killed two troopers when they tried to get water from Milk Creek. They showed off the bloody uniforms of the cavalrymen they'd mowed down in the initial attack. Then they told of the Black soldiers who'd sneaked in during the night to join the besieged troops. These men were outnumbered by the Utes and didn't dare try an attack, but the braves bragged and made fun of them, calling them "Maricat'z." Josephine later recalled that one of these Utes' "favorite amusements was to put on a Negro soldier's cap, a short coat, and blue pants, and imitate the Negroes in speech and talk." She was surprised that the Indians could mimic their dialect perfectly. Josephine said the Utes sang the sorrowful "old Negro spiritual, 'Swing low sweet chariot, Comin' for to carry me home,'" copying the melancholy tones of the voices of the Buffalo Soldiers.

Before these braves left the camp to return to Milk Creek, they held an elaborate celebration, which Josephine later described: "They made a pile of sage brush as large as a washstand and put the bloody soldier's clothes and a hat on the pile. Then they sang and did a war dance around it." For this performance, she said the Utes dressed in their finest beaded, fringed buckskin shirts, deerskin moccasins, and fur caps made of skunk and grizzly bear skins ornamented with eagle feathers. Josephine continued, "Two or three men began the dance, and the others joined in until a ring as large as a house was formed. There were some squaws dancing, and all of them had knives. They suddenly charged upon the pile of uniforms with their knives, and pretended that they were slashing and burning the brush. They became almost insane with frenzy and excitement. Their dancing lasted from 2 o'clock until sundown. Then they took the uniforms and left."

On October 11, when Colonel Merritt and his troops reached the White River Agency, they were shocked by the death and destruction. The bodies of Meeker and his 11 employees were strewn about and in poor condition, since they'd been dead for days, lying out in the open. Meeker's old friend from New York, William Post, had been shot and had fallen in the open storehouse door, a 35-pound sack of flour clutched in his arms. Nearby were the bullet-riddled bodies of young Fred Shepard and Harry Dresser, who had often brightened agency evenings with his fiddle tunes. Farm worker George Eaton's face had been so badly chewed by animals that he was almost unrecognizable. Arthur Thompson lay dead with his rifle beside him, and the body of the blacksmith, Shadrach Price, Flora's husband, was nearby. They found young Frank Dresser inside the entrance of a nearby abandoned coal mine, where he'd tried to hide. He had bullet wounds in his chest and leg, and he was clutching a sad farewell message he'd written to his mother before dying. Meeker's body was lying near his charred office, stripped of his pants and boots, and with a logging chain wrapped around his neck. He'd been shot in the head, and his skull was bashed in. A wooden barrel stave had been shoved down his throat—stark evidence of the Utes' fury at his numerous threats and lies.

The agency's American flag fluttered from the flagpole over this chaos and ruin, where nothing was left but piles of ashes and rubble. The splintered storeroom door hung open, its shelves emptied of prized rations, with its supplies wasted. Bags of grain and corn were ripped open and scattered to the winds, and tons of flour had been poured out, covering the ground like snow. The furious Utes had smashed and broken everything they laid their hands on—wagons were burned; the hated plows and mowers were smashed; washtubs, tools, and supplies destroyed. Hardware was tossed about, and what couldn't be demolished had been piled up and set on fire.

Colonel Merritt put his men to work burying the massacre victims as news of the Milk Creek battle and the massacre at the White River Agency electrified the nation. There was a great deal of concern about the welfare of the captives, and General Sheridan ordered so many troops sent to Rawlins that Union Pacific turned over the railroad for military transportation. Four days after Merritt reached the White River Agency, his forces were increased to about 900 troops. Fearing a general Ute uprising, General Crook sent additional troops from Fort Robinson, Nebraska, to Rawlins in the event Colonel Merritt needed more reinforcements. General Sheridan moved 650 cavalry troops and infantrymen, numerous Cheyenne scouts, and pack trains of supplies from New Mexico and Texas to Fort Garland. These troops were to keep a close eye on Ignacio and the Southern Utes. Sheridan alerted army posts in Utah, Dakota, Arizona,

The agency's American flag fluttered from the flagpole over chaos and ruin, and nothing was left but piles of ashes and rubble. *Courtesy of Tom Williams.*

and Oklahoma to be ready to move troops into Colorado at a moment's notice. He warned the commanders, without having any evidence, that he expected the Shoshone and Southern Utes to come to the aid of the White River Utes, who were led by Jack, Douglas, and Colorow.

Governor Pitkin wanted war with the Utes and continued to stir up trouble, falsely insisting that Ouray's band of Uncompahgre Utes had participated in the siege at Milk Creek. Releasing a letter to the Denver papers, he offered to resolve matters quickly by using the Colorado Militia. The October 1, 1879 issue of the *New York Times* observed that "Colorado's leading citizens seemed more anxious for a general Indian war than for the surrender of the captives…and the murderers of Thornburgh."

Colonel Merritt and his troops left the agency and headed south toward the mountains in pursuit of Chief Douglas and his captives. The military was ready and eager to press their advantage over the Utes to secure the women's release and punish these Indians. General Sheridan wired Colonel Merritt that if the Utes did not surrender unconditionally, "They will be exterminated.…The attack on Major Thornburgh was a piece of the basest treachery and we will respond." At first, Merritt and his troops made good time, until they encountered a dense forest of aspen, which completely blocked their caravan of supply wagons and pack mules. The troopers set to work chopping down hundreds of trees and constructing a road so the heavy wagons could pass through without getting stuck. Their work stopped when a messenger arrived from the War Department, directing Merritt to end the pursuit of the Utes because negotiations were underway for the return of the captives. Secretary of the Interior Schurz had stepped in to stop the wholescale military punishment favored by both Generals Sheridan and Sherman. He convinced both officers to try negotiations first. Then he selected a respected, former Indian agent, Charles Adams, to start working to obtain the peaceful release of the women.

Colonel Merritt was aggravated by this decision and fumed about the contradiction between "being equipped for a campaign by one arm of the government and halted in its execution by another arm of the same government." He said this was happening "on the verge of winter in a country where all campaigning very shortly will be beyond human execution." General Sheridan shared these feelings, angrily complaining that he had 1,500 to 1,600 men at the White River Agency, who were dependent on supplies from "a long and difficult road to a railhead that would soon be closed by winter snow." He continued, saying that the army had gone to White River at the request of the Indian Bureau, but "now we are left in the heart of the mountains and our hands are tied with the danger of being snowed in staring us in the face." He reminded the Secretary of the Interior that "the lives of the captives are hanging in the balance."

General Sheridan blamed the agency tragedy on the "savages." He conceded that Meeker might have precipitated the trouble by "his mismanagement and ignorance of the Indian character" and the implementation of his inappropriate "ironclad…industrial theories." But he concluded that the blame rested "on the savages who know nothing but war and the chase." Sheridan called for an all-out attack against the White River renegades and included other Ute bands and any Indians who came to their assistance. He insisted that only an unconditional surrender should be accepted. While Merritt was waiting for a resolution to the hostage negotiations, he selected a site for the new White River Agency and put his troops to work making adobe bricks and building the new post. It would be called the Cantonment at White River. President Hayes ordered the army to remain at this post while negotiations were underway for the release of the captives.

Charles Adams, the special hostage negotiator, arrived in Colorado and, with Ouray's help, located the renegade Utes' mountain hideaway on October 21. At first, the chiefs were hostile and refused to discuss the release of the women, who'd been hidden and were kept out of sight. Adams talked for hours with the chiefs and leaders, who angrily insisted that both Meeker and Thornburgh had broken promises, which led to the deaths of many. They knew that the government had assembled a large body of troops in Colorado, ready to attack, but Adams promised this military threat would end once the women were released.

The following morning, negotiations resumed, and finally, after many hours of frustration, aggrieved Indian complaints, demands, and recriminations, the Utes agreed to release their prisoners if Adams stopped the military reprisals. Adams agreed, and the three women were finally freed after being held captive by the Utes for 23 days. The eastern press was jubilant when the women left the Ute camp with Adams and expressed thanks that a peaceful solution had been found, avoiding a full-scale war. In Colorado, there was a great deal of anger over the attacks and kidnappings. A spokesman for the Lake City militia expressed the feelings of many when he said, "If the government would let us get at 'em, we'd clean 'em up in a month and make good Indians of every one of them like Chivington did with the Cheyenne" (meaning dead, like the Sand Creek Massacre). There was no sympathy for the Utes in Colorado, and Governor Pitkin urged

Colonel Merritt's troops had to build barracks at the new Cantonment at White River and endured a frigid, brutal winter with wind whistling through their flimsy tents. *Courtesy of Tom Williams.*

citizens living near Ute reservations to form their own armed militia units. Angry citizens condemned Washington for its failure to order the military to "exterminate" the Utes and for telling white settlers that they must stop trespassing on Ute reservations.

Since the barracks weren't completed at the new Cantonment at White River, many of Merritt's troops were living in tents and makeshift shelters.

They endured the frigid, brutal winter weather as the wind whistled through their flimsy tents, and blizzards piled drifts of snow on the new parade ground. In July 1880, they were replaced by six companies of the Sixth Infantry, who hoped for a more comfortable winter in 1880–81 as the post neared completion.

General Hatch and 450 Buffalo Soldiers of the Ninth Cavalry returned to Fort Garland from New Mexico in 1880. They were familiar with the Southern Utes and their leader, Ignacio, who was described as "surly and ill-tempered" by Colonel Hatch. These troops went to Animas City on the LaPlata River in southwestern Colorado, where they cleared the land and got busy building a small post called Camp Animas. It would protect Animas City, the bustling young community that supplied food and equipment to the booming mining camps in the San Juan Mountains. Shopkeepers and businessmen at Animas City were very pleased to have the Buffalo Soldiers spending money in their town. The Denver and Rio Grande Railroad was laying tracks just a few miles from Animas City, and negotiations were underway with the town fathers for land for a depot. About 500 men of the Ninth Cavalry and the Fifteenth, Nineteenth, and Twentieth Infantries would be at this new post until the "Ute problem" was resolved.

Meeker's refusal to even try to understand the Utes and his insistence that they give up all aspects of their former life to become farmers had a tragic outcome. The killing of Nathan Meeker dramatically ended over 200 years of efforts by the Utes to coexist peacefully with the white newcomers. Their own actions threatened their right to remain in western Colorado, which had been their home for many generations.

# 12

# "The Utes Must Go!"

The attack at Milk Creek and the killings at the White River Agency sealed the fate of the Utes. They might escape retaliation from the army, but the people of Colorado would exact a far worse punishment. All of the Utes would pay a high price for the actions of a few.

In late October 1879, Secretary of the Interior Schurz appointed a special Peace Commission to investigate the battle at Milk Creek and the White River Agency tragedy. Colonel Hatch was elected president of the commission; Chief Ouray and Charles Adams, who'd negotiated the release of the captives, were members; and Lieutenant Valois of Ninth Cavalry was the recorder. The commission was to identify the Utes who had murdered Nathan Meeker, his employees, and the teamsters and destroyed the agency.

Charles Adams obtained testimony from Josephine and Arvilla Meeker and Flora Price in their Greeley homes, so they would not have to appear in person. The commission met at Los Pinos on November 12, 1879, in a small, drafty log building that was heated by a potbelly stove. The assembly was guarded by a detail of Buffalo Soldiers and 50 heavily armed Ute police. Testimony was taken from 25 Utes, several army officers who were at Milk Creek, and Josephine Meeker.

The Peace Commission decided that the Utes who attacked Thornburgh's troops wouldn't be charged because they were part of a military action. Adams said the battle at Milk Creek was a "fair fight," and blame wasn't placed on either side. He added that if Thornburgh had gone to the agency without his troops as planned, all the trouble could have been avoided.

Josephine Meeker, who decided to appear in person, placed the blame on the army, testifying that "if the soldiers had not come and threatened the Indians with [jail]…and threatened to kill other Indians at White River, Meeker and the others would not have been massacred." Colorow, the leader of the Utes at Milk Creek, testified that Thornburgh had started the battle, while Jack, another chief, testified that Meeker's lies were responsible for the violence.

When the commission requested the names of the Utes who were involved in the killings at the agency, there was silence. The hearings dragged on, and while there was an uneasy peace in Colorado, Governor Pitkin and his followers howled for revenge. General Sheridan tried to calm the large military force he'd assembled in the state, knowing that a single incident between the settlers and the Indians could lead to outright war. The Utes were on edge, fearful that the actions of a few would bring dire consequences to the entire tribe.

Adams decided to present the women's complete testimony from the interviews he'd conducted in their homes. He had hoped to spare them embarrassment but decided the Peace Commission needed to know the sordid details of their captivity. Adams said that all three of the women, including 64-year-old Arvilla Meeker, had been raped by their captors. He emphasized that this must be kept secret from the public. The three women named Douglas, Johnson, and Persune as their attackers, and they identified all of the Utes who'd been at the agency when the murders were committed.

On December 6, 1879, the commission identified twelve Utes, including Johnson, Douglas, and Pursune, and demanded that they surrender. Secretary Schurz ordered the Peace Commission to end its hearings and recommended to President Hayes that a treaty removing the Utes from Colorado be drafted.

Elderly Arvilla Meeker wrote a letter to a Denver newspaper editor and described the assaults by their captors in great detail. She demanded punishment of the Ute men. Once the scandalous story was out, the nation's outrage grew. Colorado newspapers and the general public called for complete extermination of the Utes, and the legislature overwhelmingly passed a resolution demanding the expulsion of the Utes from the state. Next the legislators went even further and passed a bill titled An Act for the Destruction of Indians and Skunks, which authorized the state to pay twenty-five dollars for a dead skunk or an Indian scalp. While many Coloradans favored Governor Pitkin's proposal for complete extinction of the Utes, everyone kept up the clamor to send them to Indian Territory in Oklahoma.

The House of Representatives Committee on Indian Affairs held hearings about the battle at Milk Creek and the Meeker Massacre in January 1880. After hearing testimony and deliberating, the Congressional committee determined that the 12 men should surrender, and all the Utes must leave Colorado. A nonnegotiable agreement was drawn up, relocating the White River Utes to the Uintah Reservation in eastern Utah. The Southern Ute bands would be moved to unoccupied land on the LaPlata River in southwestern Colorado. Although the Uncompahgre Utes hadn't participated in the massacre at the agency or the battle at Milk Creek, Congress decided that they had to leave Colorado, too. They would go to the 1.9-million-acre Ouray Reservation, which was carved out of vacant land next to the Uintah Reservation. This new reservation was named for Ouray, the respected Uncompahgre peace chief, who died in August 1880 of kidney disease.

Fearing a Ute uprising, Colonel Mackenzie and six companies of the Fourth Cavalry were ordered to leave Texas and head to Colorado. The troops arrived at Fort Garland on the Denver and Rio Grande Railroad, where they were joined by several infantry companies. This swelled Mackenzie's command to 1,500 troops. Since there weren't enough barracks for such a large force, the troopers erected tents outside the adobe walls of Fort Garland. They spent a cold winter there and, in the spring of 1881, were glad to begin preparations for the 200-mile march over the mountains to the Los Pinos Agency. Several hundred Ninth Cavalry Buffalo Soldiers were among this large body of troops that left the fort and marched to the Uncompahgre Valley. This military presence at the new post, the Encampment at Uncompahgre, kept peace between the Utes and the white settlers and prospectors, who were eager to see them leave Colorado.

Many Coloradans were afraid that the Ute bands would unite to resist their move to Utah. Colonel Merritt's troops remained at the new camp at White River, where additional military had been sent to keep the peace. In late August 1881, Colonel Mackenzie told the Ute leaders to round up their herds of horses, cattle, and goats and prepare for the move to Utah. Leaving Colorado in the fall disrupted the Indians' long-established habit of hunting and preparing food for the winter. The dispirited Utes said that "they would as soon die as go to Utah," and Sapinero, who'd taken Ouray's place, announced that the Uncompahgre band would not leave Colorado. Realizing that force might be necessary, Secretary of the Interior Schurz conferred with the War Department and instructed Colonel Mackenzie:

Reproduction of a drawing, one of several made by Frederic Remington around 1888, when he went on patrol with the Tenth Cavalry in Arizona. *Courtesy of Library of Congress.*

"if the Indians will not go without force—compel removal. If the refusal is absolute, have the military proceed at once."

Colonel Mackenzie met with the Uncompahgre chiefs, who pleaded for more time, but he held firm. He delivered an ultimatum: "I want to know if you will go or not. If you will not go of your own accord, I will make you go.

When you have sufficiently discussed this matter and arrived at a conclusion, send for me. Remember, you are to go at once." Finally, the Utes decided Mackenzie was serious and they must leave Colorado.

In the fall of 1881, at least 2,000 Ute men, women, and children started their sad journey out of Colorado, escorted by Mackenzie's troops. Following the stream that became known as Evacuation Creek, they walked west to the Colorado River, where they boarded large flat boats for the trip across. There were many tears as the Utes left the land that had been their home for many generations, one that sheltered the spirits of their forefathers.

White civilians followed the Utes closely, anxious to grab their land. General Pope was disgusted and reported, "The whites were so eager and so unrestrained by common decency that it was absolutely necessary to use military force to keep them off the reservation until the Indians were fairly gone." These "reservation jumpers" had already made numerous land claims in the mountain valleys and were busily staking out farmland at the base of the Rockies. Land developers rushed in and quickly parceled out the land in the Uncompahgre Valley. They laid out the towns of Montrose, Grand Junction, and Glenwood Springs. The Denver and Rio Grande Railroad got busy laying tracks up the Uncompahgre Valley to Grand Junction.

It took the Utes two weeks to reach the Uintah Reservation on September 13, 1881. Their arrival was greeted glumly by the Uintah Utes, who'd had no say in the decision to transplant thousands of people they did not know onto their land. They'd received no compensation for any of the land, and now they would have to share their reservation with the trouble-making White River Utes. Once the Utes were out of Colorado, Colonel Mackenzie's work was done, and he and the Fourth Cavalry headed for New Mexico Territory.

# 13

# THE BUFFALO SOLDIERS
# AND THE UTES IN UTAH

Fearing trouble between the Uintah Utes and the Colorado Utes, the War Department decided a military presence near the Uintah Reservation could deter problems and approved the construction of a fort. Work was started in 1881 but never completed, due to difficulty getting building materials to the site. In 1884, the War Department abandoned the project completely.

The Ninth Cavalry had battled Apaches in the New Mexico Territory and seen action against the Utes at Milk Creek in 1879. These Buffalo Soldiers had been riding more than 350 miles a month for many years. In his annual report to Secretary of War Ramsey, General Pope noted, "These troops have been almost continuously in the field." In 1880, the Black regimental companies were sent to several different posts in Kansas, Wyoming, Nebraska, and Indian Territory to give the soldiers some relief. Unfortunately, the easiest garrison duty for the six companies of the Ninth Cavalry that went to Fort Riley, Kansas, didn't last, and these disappointed Buffalo Soldiers were soon on their way to patrol the state's southern border. Their task was to prevent white settlers, called "Boomers," from illegally crossing from Kansas into Indian Territory. These trespassers were determined to claim and homestead a 2-million-acre strip of land called "Unassigned Lands," which had been set aside for additional Indian reservations.

Keeping more than 2,000 land-hungry Boomers out of Indian Territory was a thankless task. Settlers boldly crossed the border, staked claims for farms, put up structures, and plowed their fields in the Unassigned Lands. The Twenty-Fifth Infantry joined the Ninth Cavalry in tracking down and arresting the Boomers. Then these settlers were escorted to the Kansas state line and released. Once the soldiers left, the Boomers stubbornly returned to the Unassigned Lands, and the dreary events repeated themselves. This situation became volatile when the white settlers insulted and attacked the Black soldiers and even threatened their white officers.

During the frigid winter of 1884–85, the coldest in a decade, the Ninth Cavalry pushed through the Unassigned Lands, clearing out the Boomers, and marching them back into Kansas. First Lieutenant Patrick Cusack, who served with these Buffalo Soldiers for 16 years, wrote, "This was one of the worst marches I ever experienced in the service. Although the company suffered severely, I never heard a man grumble or make any complaint." He continued, "Benjamin Bolt's horse fell through the ice crossing a stream, leaving him in wet clothes, fifteen miles from camp: he only mentioned the incident 20 years later when he filed for a military pension because of his rheumatism." Private Frank Marshall recalled that miserable winter, saying, "Nearly all the party were frozen, some more and some less." In June 1885, the Ninth Cavalry was transferred from Kansas to Fort Robinson, Nebraska, and Fort McKinney, Wyoming. The dispute over the Unassigned Lands did not end until April 1889, when President Benjamin Harrison signed an act opening the region for white settlement.

During the winter of 1885–86, there was trouble between the Ute bands, and the War Department decided again that a post was needed near the Uintah Reservation. In August 1886, General Crook selected the site, and two companies of Buffalo Soldiers, about 75 men, were transferred from Nebraska to build the new post, which was named Fort Duchesne, near the river of the same name.

Three companies of the Twenty-First Infantry rode 350 miles from Fort Steele, Wyoming, to the building site. They were joined by another infantry company from Fort Robinson. These troops narrowly missed being ambushed by more than 300 Utes, who had hidden in ravines along the road leading to the fort site. An alert scout saw the Indians' trap and warned the commander, who quickly diverted his men away from the road. When these infantrymen arrived at the building site, they were confronted by more than 700 angry Uintah and White River Utes. While some troopers stood guard with rifles ready, others quickly dug protective trenches and established

Taken in December 1890 at Fort Keogh, Montana. The Twenty-Fifth Infantry was glad to leave the hot climate of Texas after ten years and wore buffalo robes to keep warm. *Courtesy of National Archives.*

picket lines. The angry Utes finally backed off, and sentries were posted. For three tense days, the infantrymen anxiously watched the road, awaiting the arrival of the Ninth Cavalry.

Finally, distant dust clouds signaled the approach of the troops, and when Major Benteen and the Buffalo Soldiers galloped into sight, they were greeted with relieved cheers and shouts. Benteen, who would command the new fort, and two Ninth Cavalry troops had ridden 650 miles from Fort McKinney, Wyoming. They brought much-needed ammunition, supplies, and a Hotchkiss mountain gun. The Utes weren't pleased to see that Hotchkiss gun, an air-cooled, gas-operated type of machine gun, and Chief Sour of the Uintahs was very angry. He'd assumed the cavalry would be made up of white men, and he was infuriated when he saw the Black Buffalo Soldiers. He raced to the Indian agent, yelling, "All over black! All over black! Buffalo Soldiers! Wooly head! Wooly Head! Don't like them! Black white man!" Some of these White River Utes had been at Milk Creek in 1879 and remembered the Buffalo Soldiers, who'd rescued Thornburgh's troops. They shouted angrily, "Buffalo Soldiers! Buffalo Soldiers! Don't let them come!" The Uncompahgre Utes who'd lost their all their lands, even though they hadn't been part of the uprising, were angry, too. They joined the White River band, shouting, "Bad! Very Bad!" at the Black troops. The

The Ninth Cavalry traveled 650 miles from Fort McKinney in Wyoming Territory in record time, bringing much-needed ammunition and supplies and a Hotchkiss mountain gun. *Courtesy of Tom Williams.*

Indian agent calmed the irate Utes, assuring them that these Black soldiers would build a fort to protect them from the white settlers and keep peace between the Ute bands. They would also protect the eastern Utah frontier, western Colorado, and southwestern Wyoming.

Major Benteen put his troops, which consisted of 20 officers and 266 enlisted men, to work planning the fort's design, laying out the site, and making adobe bricks. They built barracks for both enlisted men and officers, a commissary, a hospital, a storehouse, and stables. Unfortunately, none of the barracks were completed before the blizzards began, so the soldiers spent the first winter in canvas tents warmed by potbellied stoves. In March 1887, they were finally able to escape the cold and move into the first completed barracks of new Fort Duchesne.

Bathing facilities at the fort were limited, and the post surgeon reported that "the lack of bath tubs, lack of conventional means of heating, and lack of privacy makes bathing very uncomfortable, so it is frequently neglected." A soldier who wanted a bath had to settle for a cold plunge into the nearby "mosquito infested, rocky bottomed Duchesne River." Since military wives were allowed at this post, the major welcomed Mrs. Benteen, the spouses of his four officers, and the wives of three Buffalo Soldiers, who became the post's laundresses.

Major Benteen had survived the Battle of the Little Big Horn in 1876 and had taken part in the campaign against Chief Joseph and the Nez Perce Indians in 1877. He was promoted to major in 1882 and transferred to the Ninth Cavalry, although he made no secret of the fact that he did not like Black soldiers. He was frequently abusive, swearing and using foul language toward the Buffalo Soldiers. He said he "took no interest in this race of troops on account of their low-down, rascally character." Despite Major Benteen's attitude, the Buffalo Soldiers and the white troops got along well at Fort Duchesne.

Major Benteen disliked everyone, especially the Mormon settlers. He said, "Some think I came here to fight Indians, but I came here to fight Mormons." He cursed at Mormon settlers and always tried to pick a fight with the men. Once in a drunken rage, he pulled his revolver on the Uintah County sheriff and would have shot him if another officer hadn't grabbed his gun. Benteen drank so heavily that he was suspended in December 1886, but he was soon reinstated. In 1887, he was suspended for drunk and disorderly conduct, court-martialed, convicted, and faced dismissal from the army, until President Cleveland intervened and reduced his sentence. Frederick Benteen retired on July 7, 1888, and died four years later.

The nomadic Utes retained their hunting rights in Colorado, and every fall, large groups returned to hunt game for their winter food supply. The Utes enjoyed their fall trips and came with their wives, children, ponies, dogs, and even their goats. The men and their families crowded the narrow streets of the small Colorado settlements when they came to trade. Businessmen welcomed them, seeing an opportunity to make money, but many frightened citizens just wanted them to leave. The Utes usually brought their fastest horses to race against the local cowboys. Crowds came to bet on their favorites, but the smart gamblers put their money on the Utes' swift ponies. The wives of ranchers, farmers, and merchants tried to keep their husbands away from these sporting events because the speedy Indian horses usually crossed the finish line first and ran away with all the prize money.

In 1893, the elegant Hotel Colorado, featuring a luxurious spa with vapor caves and hot springs, once a favorite of the Utes, opened in Glenwood Springs. The hotel built a polo field, where its wealthy, polo-playing guests from the East, mounted on Thoroughbreds, pitted their skills against the local cowboys, who rode swift, tough Ute ponies. The cowboys were usually the victors in these contests and made money selling their fast Indian horses to these visitors. Excited polo enthusiasts loaded their new mounts on the Denver & Rio Grande Railroad for the journey back home, where they defeated their astonished competitors on the polo fields.

The Utes' annual hunting trips to Colorado were interrupted in 1887, when the state hired game wardens to enforce its new hunting laws. The Indian hunting parties sometimes killed a great many animals for their winter food supply, angering Coloradans, who had to follow the limits imposed by their new laws. When game wardens raided the Ute hunting camps, trouble usually resulted, with injuries on both sides. Ute women, who were gathering berries, were often heckled and frightened by cowboys; a sheriff's posse tore up the camp of women preparing meat and tanning hides. This began a series of confrontations between the Utes and local law enforcement, which became known as Colorow's War.

In August 1887, the sheriff of Garfield County entered the hunting camp where Chipeta, Ouray's widow, and several women, children, and old men were preparing food for winter. When the sheriff ordered them to leave, Chipeta refused, saying that all treaties gave the Utes the right to be there. The sheriff grew angry, and his men threatened the group, frightening them until they fled and hid in the brush. Hours later, they returned to find their camp burned, and their meat and food stores destroyed.

In late August, Colorow and a group of sub-chiefs were enjoying a rejuvenating soak in the mineral waters near Glenwood Springs when county sheriff Jim Kendall and a large posse galloped up. The sheriff accused Colorow of stealing horses and threatened to arrest him. The Ute denied the charge and, moving rapidly, hopped out of the hot springs. He leaped on his horse and made his getaway, followed by the others. Surprisingly, no one was shot, and Colorow and the others headed toward the Utah border. They were met by Captain Wright and a troop of Buffalo Soldiers from Fort Duchesne, who escorted them back to their reservation.

Later that fall, Colorow and a large band of Utes returned to hunt in northwestern Colorado, and again, Sheriff Kendall and a posse of rough cowboys stormed into their camp and accused two Utes of stealing horses. A fierce argument led to gunfire, and the Utes fled in a hail of bullets. No one was injured, but Sheriff Kendall started a rumor that the Utes were on the warpath. Frightened farmers and ranchers poured into the little settlement of Meeker for protection; the agitated mayor sent a telegram to the governor for troops to prevent a massacre. Seven Colorado National Guard units took the train from Denver to Meeker and joined the Aspen Militia and a battalion of Leadville volunteers. Sheriff Kendall recruited a posse of about 75 cowboys and ranchers who were anxious to chase down those Ute horse thieves. This excited army of volunteers, led by Kendall, galloped out of town, eager for a fight.

When Colorow learned a large posse was pursuing his hunting party, he made a wise decision and headed for the safety of the Utah reservation. The Utes had a large herd of horses with them so they could change mounts when their animals tired, but the posse members had only one horse apiece. After four days of hard riding, the posse hadn't caught the Utes, and their horses were worn out. Kendall's excited cowboys were getting hungry, too, because they'd dashed out of town without packing enough provisions.

One evening, the Utes decided to make a stand near the Colorado-Utah border. They concealed themselves in the rocky bluffs overlooking a trail through a large meadow. The Indians spent the night waiting for the posse to appear. Just as the sun rose the following morning, the tired cowboys and a few members of the National Guard rode into the meadow, and the Utes began firing. When they saw the military uniforms of the National Guard, they stopped shooting and began waving a white flag, since they didn't want a battle with the army. Colorow sent a messenger carrying the white flag to talk with the sheriff, but a trigger-happy cowboy started shooting and wounded the messenger. There was heavy gunfire from the Utes in retaliation. The battle went on for hours, and as daylight faded, the Utes stealthily moved out of the rocks. They retrieved their hidden horses and quietly rode off toward the Utah border. Despite being wounded, Colorow got on his horse and managed to keep up with the others.

Two militia members were killed in the skirmish, and there were several wounded. The rest of the posse, led by Kendall, resumed the chase. When word of the trouble in Colorado reached Fort Duchesne, First Lieutenant George Burnett and ten Buffalo Soldiers saddled up and galloped to the border. The troops, positioned strategically along the state line, waited with their weapons drawn and ready. They saw the cloud of dust as the Utes approached rapidly with the huge posse right behind them. As Colorow and the Utes drew near, the Buffalo Soldiers quickly moved aside to let them dash through the opening, and then closed ranks as the posse galloped toward them. The sheriff suddenly realized that these Buffalo Soldiers were not going to move aside, and he started screaming, "Halt! Halt!" The cowboys and National Guardsmen frantically pulled and sawed on their reins, bringing their horses to sliding stops. Clouds of dust billowed about, and curses filled the air. Nose to nose with the shouting sheriff, angry cowboys, and the militia, Lieutenant Burnett and the ten Buffalo Soldiers stood their ground. When the sheriff calmed down and stopped yelling threats, the lieutenant quietly told him and the National Guardsmen that they had no authority in Utah or on the Uintah Reservation. After making plenty of ominous promises about the lieutenant's future, the disgusted posse turned around and headed back to Colorado.

Indian agent T.A. Byrnes, who'd accompanied the troops, wrote a letter to the Commissioner of Indian Affairs praising the lieutenant's handling of the explosive situation. He commended the ten Buffalo Soldiers for the "exceptional courage and bravery" they'd shown when they were greatly outnumbered by the angry cowboys and militiamen. News of the incident and the Utes' perilous escape from the posse circulated around the reservation. Colorow told everyone how the Buffalo Soldiers and the lieutenant had saved him and the others from certain death at the hands of the posse. The Utes formed new, favorable opinions of the Buffalo Soldiers whom they'd scornfully called "white men with black faces." Camaraderie and respect between the Indians and the Black soldiers increased and made the environment more pleasant for everyone.

There were jokes about "Colorow's War," but it wasn't funny to the old chief, who continued to suffer from the wounds he received on this last trip to Colorado. Colorow's condition worsened, and he died in late 1888 on the reservation in Utah. When they heard the news, many pioneer wives in Colorado recalled his surprise visits and biscuit-begging forays into their kitchens. Colorow's War is believed to be the last conflict between Native Americans and whites in Colorado.

In 1896, the entire Twenty-Fourth Infantry was assembled at Fort Douglas, the first time in the regiment's 27-year history that all of its soldiers were at the same location. This post was on the edge of Salt Lake City, and it was the Buffalo Soldiers' first assignment in an urban area instead of a remote, undeveloped territory. At first, Salt Lake City's citizens resisted having Black troops assigned to the fort because they thought the white women would be attacked. They even lobbied their U.S. senator to have the Black troops transferred. The Buffalo Soldiers were upset by this blatant prejudice, and one private wrote to the *Salt Lake Tribune* that "his fellow soldiers objected to being classed as lawless barbarians." Another trooper assured the citizens: "You will find our regiment better behaved and disciplined than most of the white soldiers."

Families of enlisted men were welcomed at Fort Douglas, and when the wives and children arrived, Utah more than doubled its Black population.

*Left*: Families of enlisted men were welcome at Fort Douglas, and when the wives and children arrived, Utah more than doubled its Black population. *Courtesy of National Archives.*

*Below*: A twenty-man unit of Twenty-Fifth Infantry Bicycle Corps traveled from Fort Missoula, Montana, to St. Louis in an experiment on moving troops, 1896–97. *Courtesy of University of Montana Special Collection.*

The Buffalo Soldiers brought their music, bright ragtime, jazz, and spirituals, plus their enthusiasm for baseball and sports, social clubs and church services, picnics, and family activities. Their baseball team, the Colored Monarchs, played the local teams; the Twenty-Fourth Infantry Band was in demand for civic celebrations and special events. The soldiers were invited to take part in Salt Lake City's Jubilee Celebration on Pioneer Day. Their participation brought newspaper raves about the Buffalo Soldiers' "thrilling demonstrations of horsemanship, sabre skills, and marksmanship."

In 1898, after only 19 months in Utah, when the Spanish-American War began, the Twenty-Fourth Infantry was ordered to Cuba. Salt Lake City citizens turned out to bid the soldiers farewell when they left. Businesses closed, and the streets and buildings were decked out in red, white, and blue bunting. White families, who'd once been afraid to have Black soldiers in their city, lined up to shake hands with the departing men and wish them well. The governor, lieutenant governor, mayor, and city officials marched to the depot with the Buffalo Soldiers, who were accompanied by a special honor guard. The streets were jammed with crowds cheering the troops, and everyone waved enthusiastically as the train pulled out of the Salt Lake City depot.

# 14

## THE LATER YEARS

The Buffalo Soldiers of the Ninth and Tenth Cavalries, the Twenty-Fourth and Twenty-Fifth Infantries served on the western frontier from 1866 through the 1890s. They fought in the Indian Wars on the Great Plains and spent more than a decade in a bloody struggle with the Apaches in Arizona and New Mexico. They earned the respect of the Utes of Colorado and Utah and were at Pine Ridge during the last military action in the Sioux War. During more than 30 years of bloody combat, they built forts, constructed roads and bridges, and strung miles of telegraph wire. They patrolled the border, tracked down outlaws, and supported the nation's westward expansion. Despite the danger and hardships of the frontier, miserable living conditions, and inferior food, the Buffalo Soldiers served with honor.

The Black regiments were tough, disciplined fighting units with high morale and regimental pride, and their desertion rate was the lowest in the army—much lower than the white units. In 1877, after a very difficult year in Texas, Colonel Grierson's Tenth Cavalry had 18 desertions, compared to Colonel Mackenzie's white Fourth Cavalry, which had 184. While fighting Apaches in New Mexico Territory and controlling the Utes in Colorado, the Ninth Cavalry had 6 desertions, compared to 172 for the Seventh Cavalry. The Black troops did not take refuge in alcohol, the scourge of the army, and their courage and determination earned the respect of their officers and fellow soldiers.

White officers who'd refused to accept a command with Black troops in 1866 changed their mind after seeing the Buffalo Soldiers' courage and fighting ability. In 1878, a West Point graduate, who'd been working with both white and Black infantry companies, wrote home, "It does not take long for one to change entirely his ideas in respect to these troops. They make excellent soldiers." An indication of the growing respect among the military for the Black troops was the increasing number of high-ranking West Point graduates who chose to serve with the Ninth and Tenth Cavalry between 1877 and 1891.

Colonel Zenas Bliss, who served with both the Twenty-Fourth and Twenty-Fifth Infantries during the turbulent times in Texas, praised the "many gallant deeds" of the Black troopers. He spoke of their service during the Indian Wars, saying that "these men ranked among the best soldiers on the frontier." In 1870, General John Pope, commander of the Department of the Missouri, wrote, "Everything that any man could do, the Buffalo Soldiers did."

The ability of the Black soldiers to sing and joke under the most miserable conditions endeared them to their commanders. In October 1879, Lieutenant Walter Finley, pursuing the renegade Victorio in New Mexico with the Ninth Cavalry, marveled, "Darkeys are so much better on these long marches than white men. They ride along singing, and even when they lose their horses, they walk beside the column, laughing and cracking jokes as if a 40-mile walk was a mere bagatelle [game]."

Four troops of the Ninth Cavalry were sent to the Pine Ridge Agency in November 1890, but they were not involved in the Massacre at Wounded Knee on December 29, 1890. This fight was between the Sioux and the Seventh Cavalry. The following day, some troops of the Seventh Cavalry were attacked and pinned down in a valley by another band of Sioux. These men were rescued by a battalion of the Ninth Cavalry, whose sudden wild charge surprised the Indians and drove them off. These Buffalo Soldiers, commanded by Major Guy Henry, remained at Wounded Knee until March 1891, spending the frigid winter nights sleeping on the ground in canvas tents. There were 15 men in each tent, which was heated by a single, small stove. This wasn't adequate in the subzero weather as howling winds and fierce blizzards piled up 20-foot-high snowdrifts. The men crowded their horses inside the tents to keep them warm and chased off longhorn steers that plowed in seeking warmth. Years later, an article in the December 26, 1896 issue of *Harper's Weekly* described those miserable conditions: "The men's commanders were astounded by their ability to settle down in their

Member of the Ninth Cavalry Pine Ridge Agency in December 1890. The Ninth Cavalry didn't participate in Battle at Wounded Knee but rescued the Seventh Cavalry from Sioux attack on December 30, 1890. *Courtesy of Kansas Historical Society.*

crowded tents to have a good time each evening after a Spartan repast of bread and coffee, and sometimes a little bacon. Song and story, with an occasional jig or a selection on the mouth organ or the banjo occupied the night hours till taps sounded for bed, and then the morning revile [*sic*]… seemed to find these jolly fellows still laughing."

In late March, Major Henry finally obtained the army's permission to transfer his men to Fort Robinson, Nebraska, where they would have shelter in warm barracks. They set out on the 70-mile march to the fort, but a sudden blizzard blew up, making travel nearly impossible. Henry hurried his exhausted troops along until they reached a small town, where he rented an ice-skating rink to shelter the men and their horses from the storm. By the next morning, the blizzard had abated a bit, so the Buffalo Soldiers began one of the most difficult marches they ever made. They had to break their way through deep drifts, and the trail was often obscured by snow. The exhausted men plodded along, though many were ill with influenza, and most were snow-blind. Their faces were blistered and burned so badly from the snow's reflection and the biting wind that one man observed, "You could hardly tell the white officers from the Black privates." When they finally

reached Fort Robinson, the exhausted troops stumbled into the stables to feed their worn-out horses, gratified that there was plenty of hay and grain. Then, they fell into their bunks in the warm barracks, too exhausted to eat even a cup of soup. Wounded Knee was the final battle fought by the U.S. Cavalry in America's deadly war against the Plains Indians, and the Ninth Cavalry was the last regiment to leave Pine Ridge in 1891.

*Opposite*: Private William Cobbs, Buffalo Soldier Twenty-Fourth Infantry, 1894, Colorado. Private Cobbs and his regiment guarded Raton Pass and the railroad during the 1894 Pullman Railroad Strike. The private had his photo taken by a local photographer. *Courtesy History Colorado.*

*Right*: Buffalo Soldiers ready for action in Cuba in 1898 during the Spanish-American War. These troops led the charge up San Juan Hill with Roosevelt's Rough Riders. *Courtesy of Library of Congress.*

The Buffalo Soldiers served on the western frontier until the Spanish-American War, which began in 1898. Then the four Black regiments boarded ships for Cuba, where they fought at San Juan Hill with Teddy Roosevelt and the Rough Riders. More than 100 years later, military historians now say that those brave soldiers of the Ninth and Tenth Cavalries and the Twenty-Fourth and Twenty-Fifth Infantries were the first to fight to the top of Kettle and San Juan Hills, challenging Teddy Roosevelt's claim. Studies of unit maps and records of troop movements show that the Buffalo Soldiers did storm and capture San Juan Hill before Teddy Roosevelt and his volunteer Rough Riders pushed through to join them.

In the spirit of Black and white fighting side by side, Color Sergeant George Berry, who was carrying the flag of the Tenth Cavalry, picked up the colors of a fallen white soldier of the Third Cavalry and, unarmed, rushed to the top of San Juan Hill and planted the flags of both regiments. About 15,000 troops participated in the battles on these hills above Santiago, Cuba, on July 1, 1898. There were around 13,000 white soldiers and 2,000 Black. More than 200 soldiers were killed that day; of that, 30 were Buffalo Soldiers. After the Battle of San Juan Hill, Rough Rider Frank Knox said, "I never saw braver men anywhere." Lieutenant John J. "Black Jack" Pershing, who commanded a division of the Tenth in the charge up the Hill, later wrote, "They fought their way into the hearts of the American people." The Buffalo Soldiers fought in the Philippine-

Buffalo Soldiers in the Twenty-Fourth Infantry and Ninth Cavalry patrolled Sequoia and Yosemite National Parks in 1899, 1903, and 1904. Colonel Young was the first Black superintendent of a national park. *Courtesy of National Park Service.*

American Wars, which began in 1899 and lasted until 1902. Black regiments served at army posts in the West, Hawaii, the Philippines, and the Presidio of San Francisco.

The army took over the protection of Yellowstone, the nation's first National Park, in 1886 and Sequoia and Yosemite in 1891. In 1899, 1903, and 1904, troops of the Twenty-Fourth Infantry and Ninth Cavalry, approximately 500 Buffalo Soldiers, served in Yosemite National Park and nearby Sequoia. The troops at each park handled numerous duties: evicting poachers and timber thieves, constructing roads and trails, and fighting forest fires. The presence of these soldiers as official stewards of park lands brought a sense of law and order to the mountain wilderness.

Charles Young, the third Black man to graduate from the U.S. military academy at West Point, served as the acting military superintendent of Sequoia National Park in 1903. He was the first Black superintendent of a national park. Duty in the parks was unusual for these troops, and assignment in the Sierra Nevada was regarded as the Cavalryman's Paradise.

Paradise came to an end for Young and the Tenth Cavalry in 1916, when they were stationed along the border during the Mexican Revolution. On March 1916, Pancho Villa attacked the little town of Columbus, New Mexico, killed 19 people, and left their village in flames. In retaliation, General "Black Jack" Pershing, Captain Young, and the Tenth Cavalry

Many battle sites where Buffalo Soldiers fought and died are not marked, and their grave sites have been lost to time. *Courtesy of Tom Williams.*

pursued him into northern Mexico. This "Punitive Expedition of 1916" defeated Villa's forces, but the revolutionary leader managed to escape the U.S. troops. Border conflicts continued until the Tenth Cavalry and the Thirty-Fifth Infantry defeated the Mexican military in the Battle of Ambos Nogales in August 1918 on the Arizona-Mexico border.

Charles Young became the first Black man to achieve the rank of colonel and was the highest-ranking Black officer in the army until his death in 1922.

Eighteen Buffalo Soldiers, who served in the Indian Wars between 1865 and 1899, received the Medal of Honor for bravery. This is the highest honor that can be given to a member of the military for valor. Eight members of the Ninth Cavalry were honored, four men of the Tenth Cavalry received the medal, and six medals went to members of the Twenty-Fourth Infantry. During the Spanish-American War, five men in the Tenth Cavalry received the Medal of Honor.

When General Grierson, the first commander of the Tenth Cavalry, served 23 years with the regiment and was promoted to commander of the Department of Arizona, he praised the Buffalo Soldiers, saying, "Always in the vanguard of civilization and in contact with the most warlike and savage Indians of the Plains, the officers and men have cheerfully endured many hardships and privations, and in the midst of great dangers, steadfastly maintained a most gallant and zealous devotion to duty, and they may well be proud of the record made, and rest assured, that the hard work undergone in the accomplishment of such important and valuable service to their country, is well understood and appreciated, and that it cannot fail sooner or later to meet with due recognition and respect."

More than a century passed after General Grierson's call for recognition and appreciation of the service of the Buffalo Soldiers. The nation didn't learn about their legacy in the history of the West until late 1967, when William Leckie's book, *The Buffalo Soldiers,* was published. Interest in the Buffalo Soldiers grew as people learned more about the contributions

*Above*: The Tenth Cavalry with Lieutenant John "Black Jack" Pershing in Montana, carried out a large round-up of 600 Cree Indians and returned them to Canada. *Courtesy Montana Historical Society.*

*Right*: Clinton Greaves Memorial Statue in Fort Bayard, New Mexico. Greaves was awarded the Medal of Honor for bravery against Apaches in the Florida Mountains in New Mexico. *Courtesy of Tom Williams.*

Buffalo Soldier Memorial Statue at Fort Bliss, Texas, depicts a Ninth Cavalry trooper on horseback, rifle in hand, riding against Apaches during the Guadalupe Campaign. *Courtesy of Texas Travel Council.*

made by these Black men. After General Colin Powell dedicated a splendid equestrian statue of a Black cavalryman at Fort Leavenworth in 1992, more monuments and statues appeared. Museums featured displays about Buffalo Soldiers in the West, and their importance in Black history was acknowledged. Reenactment groups were formed, and Buffalo Soldiers rode proudly in parades and patriotic celebrations. Today, the Buffalo Soldiers' contribution to our nation's history is recognized, and they are taking their rightful place with America's military heroes.

# Bibliography

Billington, Monroe. *New Mexico's Buffalo Soldiers: 1866–1900.* Niwot: University Press of Colorado, 1991.

Broome, Jeff. *Dog Soldier Justice.* Lincoln: University of Nebraska Press, 2003.

Burton, Art. *Black Buckskin, and Blue.* Austin, TX: Lakin Press, 1999.

Cashin, Herschel. *Under Fire with the 10th Cavalry.* Niwot: University Press of Colorado, 1993.

Colorado Historical Society. *Fort Garland Museum.* Denver, CO: self-published, 1990.

Cozzens, Peter. *The Earth Is Weeping.* New York: Alfred Knopf, 2016.

Davis, Richard. *The Last Indian Summer.* Farmington Hills, MI: Five Star Publishing, 2015.

Dawson, F. *The Ute War.* Boulder, CO: Johnson Publishing Company, 1980.

Decker, Peter. *The Utes Must Go.* Golden, CO: Fulcrum Publishing, 2004.

Dobak, William. *The Black Regulars.* Norman: University of Oklahoma Press, 2001.

Downey, Fairfax. *The Buffalo Soldiers in the Indian Wars.* New York: McGraw Hill, 1969.

Emmitt, Robert. *The Last War Trail.* Norman: University of Oklahoma Press, 1954.

Fowler, Arlen. *The Black Infantry in the West: 1869–1891.* Norman: University of Oklahoma Press, 1971.

Gallagher, Jolie. *Colorado's Forts.* Charleston, SC: The History Press, 2013.

Frazer, Robert. *Forts of the West.* Norman: University of Oklahoma Press, 1965.

Glass, Edward. *History of the 10ᵗʰ Cavalry.* Self-published, 1923.

Glassrud, Bruce. *Buffalo Soldiers in the West.* College Station: Texas A&M University Press, 1984.

Grinnell, George. *The Fighting Cheyenne.* Emmaus, PA: JG Press, 1995.

Hyde, George. *A Life of George Bent.* Norman: University of Oklahoma Press, 1967.

Keim, De B. *Sheridan's Troops on the Borders.* Norman: University of Oklahoma Press, 1985.

Kenner, Charles. *Buffalo Soldiers and Their Officers.* Norman: University of Oklahoma Press, 1999.

Jocknick, Sydney. *Early Days on the Western Slope.* Ouray, CO: Western Reflections Publishing, 1998.

Langellier, John. *Fighting for Uncle Sam.* Atglen, PA: Schiffer Publishing, 2016.

Lavender, David. *The Big Divide.* New York: Doubleday, 1949.

Leonard, Elizabeth. *Men of Color, to Arms.* New York: W. Norton, 2010.

Marsh, Charles. *People of the Shining Mountains.* Boulder, CO: Pruett Publishing, 1982.

McCracken, Harold, ed. *Frederic Remington's Own West.* New York: Dial Publishing, 1960.

Members of the Potomac Corral of Westerners. *Great Western Indian Fights.* Self-published, 1960.

Michno, Gregory. *The Encyclopedia of Indian Wars.* Missoula, MT: Mountain Publishing, 2003.

Miller, Mark. *Hollow Victory.* Niwot: University Press of Colorado, 1997.

Meyerson, Harvey. *Nature's Army.* Lawrence: University Press of Kansas, 2001.

Pettit, Jan. *Utes: The Mountain People.* Boulder, CO: Johnson Publishing, 1990.

Rockwell, Wilson. *The Utes: A Forgotten People.* Ouray, CO: Western Reflections Publishing, 1956.

Schubert, Frank. *Black Valor: The Buffalo Soldiers and the Medal of Honor.* Wilmington, DE: Scholarly Resources Publishing, 1997.

———. *On the Trail of the Buffalo Soldiers.* Wilmington, DE: Scholarly Resources Publishing, 1995.

———. *Voices of the Buffalo Soldiers.* Albuquerque: University of New Mexico Press, 2005.

Sheffer, Debra. *The Buffalo Soldiers.* Santa Barbara, CA: Praeger Publishing, 2015.

Shellum, Brian. *Black Officer in a Buffalo Soldier Regiment.* Lincoln: University of Nebraska Press, 2010.

Silbernagel, Robert. *Troubled Trails*. Salt Lake City: University of Utah Press, 2011.

Simmons, Virginia. *The Ute Indians*. Boulder: University Press of Colorado, 2000.

Smith, W. David. *Ouray, Chief of the Utes*. Ouray, CO: Wayfinder Press, 1986.

Sprague, Marshall. *Massacre*. Lincoln: University of Nebraska Press, 1956.

Tucker, Phillip. *Cathy Williams*. Mechanicsburg, PA: Stackpole Books, 2002.

Utley, Robert. *Frontier Regulars*. Lincoln: University of Nebraska Press, 1973.

Vandenbusche, Diane. *A Land Alone: Colorado's Western Slope*. Boulder, CO: Pruett Publishing, 1981.

# Index

# ABOUT THE AUTHOR

Nancy is drawn to historic places in the West that look much as they did centuries ago. Beecher Island is a lonely spot far out on the eastern Colorado plains where little has changed. Summit Springs is so quiet you can almost hear the ghosts of those who died there on a foggy July morning in 1869. The monument at Milk Creek is worn and crumbling, but the stream still flows by where so many suffered, calling for its water. Nancy is inspired by the stories of the people who struggled to carve out a life in the West. She writes about their dreams, their endurance, and their courage.

*Visit us at*
www.historypress.com